Developing Academic Language
with the SIOP® Model

Developing Academic Language with the SIOP® Model

Deborah J. Short
Academic Language Research & Training

Jana Echevarría
California State University, Long Beach

PEARSON

Boston • Columbus • Indianapolis • New York • San Francisco • Hoboken
Amsterdam • Cape Town • Dubai • London • Madrid • Milan • Munich • Paris • Montreal • Toronto
Delhi • Mexico City • Sao Paulo • Sydney • Hong Kong • Seoul • Singapore • Taipei • Tokyo

Vice President and Editorial Director: Jeffery W. Johnston
Senior Acquisitions Editor: Julie Peters
Program Manager: Megan Moffo
Project Manager: Mary Beth Finch
Editorial Assistant: Andrea Hall
Executive Field Marketing Manager: Krista Clark
Executive Product Marketing Manager: Christopher Barry
Procurement Specialist: Deidra Skahill
Senior Art Director: Diane Lorenzo
Text Designer: Cenveo® Publisher Services
Cover Designer: Jennifer Hart Design
Cover Art: Rebecca Emery, Getty Images
Media Project Manager: Allison Longley
Full-Service Project Management: Cenveo® Publisher Services
Composition: Cenveo® Publisher Services
Printer/Binder: RR Donnelley
Cover Printer: RR Donnelley
Text Font: 10.5/14 Times Roman

Credits and acknowledgments for material borrowed from other sources and reproduced, with permission, in this textbook appear on the appropriate page within the text.

Every effort has been made to provide accurate and current Internet information in this book. However, the Internet and information posted on it are constantly changing, so it is inevitable that some of the Internet addresses listed in this textbook will change.

Library of Congress Cataloging-in-Publication Data is on file with the Library of Congress.

ISBN 10: 0-13-708524-9
ISBN 13: 978-0-13-708524-8

For the learners who strive to improve their English every day and their teachers who support them each step of the way.

About the Authors

Deborah J. Short, Ph.D., directs Academic Language Research & Training and provides professional development on academic literacy, content-based ESL, and sheltered instruction worldwide. Formerly, she was a Division Director at the Center for Applied Linguistics where she co-developed the research-validated SIOP® Model. She has directed research studies on English learners for the Carnegie Corporation of New York, Rockefeller Foundation, and United States Department of Education, among others. Publications include professional journal articles, SIOP® Model books, and ESL textbooks for National Geographic Learning/Cengage. She taught English as a second/foreign language in New York, California, Virginia, and the Democratic Republic of the Congo.

Jana Echevarría is Professor Emerita of Education at California State University, Long Beach, where she was selected as Outstanding Professor. She has taught in elementary, middle, and high school in general education, special education, ESL, and bilingual programs. She has lived in Taiwan, Spain, and Mexico where she taught and conducted research. Her UCLA doctorate earned her an award from the National Association for Bilingual Education's Outstanding Dissertations Competition, and subsequent research and publications focus on effective instruction for English learners, including those with learning disabilities. She has presented her research across the U.S. and internationally including Oxford University (England), Wits University (South Africa), Harvard University (U.S.), South East Europe University (Macedonia), and University of Barcelona (Spain). Publications include the popular SIOP® book series and over 50 books, book chapters, and journal articles.

Contents

Academic language is a hot topic. And not just for teachers of English learners. With increased rigor and high academic standards in schools, there is growing awareness that all students benefit from attention to the language demands of academic tasks, texts, and discussions. Currently, educators are giving much more consideration to the level of language required in lessons such as the complex vocabulary, sentence structure, and academic expressions that students need to complete assignments successfully. However, English learners are learning the same challenging material and complex language as English proficient students, but they are doing it through a second language. It is because of the situation faced by English learners that we wrote this book.

Although this book is intended for all educators, many of you are already familiar with our work with the SIOP Model (Echevarría, Vogt, & Short, 2000; 2013). Twenty years ago we developed an approach to lesson planning and delivery that focuses specifically on the academic and linguistic needs of English learners. The SIOP Model, whose features are seen in Appendix A, is a framework that shows teachers how to integrate language and content instruction and identifies key elements that should be in every lesson delivered to students learning content through a new language. Used widely across the United States, the SIOP Model has been shown to improve academic outcomes for English learners (Short, Echevarría, & Richards-Tutor, 2011). You will see references to the SIOP Model throughout this book, particularly in Chapter 2. The reason is that the SIOP Model reflects best practices for English learners based on decades of research on second language acquisition and effective instruction, as well as on the SIOP Model itself. As an illustration of its relevance to this book, more than half of the features of the SIOP Model focus on academic language development.

Developing Academic Language offers educators an in-depth look at what academic language is and recommends ways for teachers to encourage and advance English learners' language proficiency and academic performance. It is a comprehensive approach for identifying students' areas of need and using a variety of techniques for improving English learners' language proficiency.

Overview of This Book

This book examines various aspects of language that require attention and focused instruction for developing academic English. Our intent is that teachers use a consistent and systematic approach for implementing the ideas presented in the chapters.

Chapter 1 Understanding Academic Language: A Second Language for All

As the title implies, in this chapter we define academic language and how it impacts English-speaking students and English learners alike in school settings. The chapter also addresses what teachers need to know about teaching academic English to English learners.

Chapter 2 Maximizing Language Development in Lessons

In this chapter we provide information to help teachers anticipate when and where language learning can and should take place in SIOP lessons. Specifically we walk through the SIOP components and identify the features where academic language development is paramount and explain how to maximize the language learning in the lessons.

Chapter 3 Strengthening Language Objectives

In this chapter, we highlight the importance of including language objectives in all lessons so that students can develop and strengthen the language and literacy skills they need for academic success. In order for this to happen, teachers must plan carefully, teach explicitly to the language objectives, and offer multiple opportunities for academic language practice. This chapter offers specific steps for identifying and writing language objectives too.

Chapter 4 Building Academic Vocabulary

This chapter and Chapter 5 both focus on aspects of academic language that are critically important for English learners to acquire: vocabulary and oral language. These are two areas where English learners have a significant knowledge gap when compared to English speakers since they did not grow up learning English as their first language. In Chapter 4 we present a plethora of ideas for strengthening vocabulary development to ensure that students are actively building their knowledge in every lesson.

Chapter 5 Enhancing Academic Oral Language

In this chapter we emphasize the need for opportunities to develop oral language. English learners have had much less exposure to the sounds, words, and phrases of English than their English-speaking peers and far fewer opportunities to develop an innate sense of English grammar. So, as with vocabulary development (Chapter 4), teachers need to help our English learners catch up by providing explicit instruction in the listening and speaking skills needed in an academic classroom environment.

Chapter 6 Promoting Collaborative Academic Discussions

This chapter builds on the discussion of oral language in Chapter 5 and takes those practices one step further to enable students to participate in rich, academic discussions. The suggestions we offer are not simply for classes with English learners; they will apply to all classrooms where productive student talk can be enhanced.

Chapter 7 Advancing Academic Language Proficiency

In this chapter we focus on those students who have seemingly plateaued in their language development, at a high intermediate or advanced level overall, yet are still considered English learners or struggling readers or writers by district guidelines. We offer some guidance for assessing gaps in students' knowledge and then addressing those gaps.

Features of the Book

- Learning Outcomes—each chapter begins with content and language objectives, which are the hallmark of the SIOP Model. The objectives provide focus for readers and help them identify specific knowledge they will gain from the chapter.

- Tools for Practice—to augment information in the chapters, we present a variety of tools throughout the book such as lists of guidelines and procedures, examples of sentence frames, sentence starters and scripts, and other devices to assist in making the information more concrete for readers.

- Application Activities—each chapter presents opportunities for readers to apply the chapter's information so that it is relevant to their own teaching situation.

- Links to Common Core State Standards and other state standards—we recognize that not all states have adopted the CCSS, but all states have standards that are challenging for English learners to achieve. Across the United States, academic standards share many common themes and skills, and in each chapter we present specific ideas for advancing students' academic language in order to meet state standards.

- End-of-Chapter Summary—each chapter has a concluding section that summarizes the main points using a bulleted list. Readers can easily review the chapter's information with the summary.

- Questions for Reflection—Individual readers, book study groups, and university classes alike will find the questions a useful way to think more deeply about the chapter's material.

Acknowledgments

As with any undertaking such as this book, we are indebted to colleagues and teachers who have influenced our thinking along the way. In particular, we wish to recognize our friend and collaborator, Dr. MaryEllen Vogt, who is a co-developer of the SIOP Model and has been a valued colleague for many years. Also, we are grateful to Amy Washam, who is an outstanding SIOP trainer, colleague, and friend. A huge thank you goes to Aurora Martinez Ramos for her vision, patience, and persistence in shepherding this book along. Finally, we appreciate the contributions of the generous SIOP teachers in Norwalk, Connecticut who gave us access to their classrooms and shared their ideas.

We would also like to thank our reviewers: Margaret E. D. Baker, Whitfield County Schools; Katharine Garcia, University of St. Thomas; and Laurie Weaver, University of Houston-Clear Lake.

1

Understanding Academic Language: A Second Language for All

amyinlondon/Fotolia

Complete the matching exercise. Can you match Column A with Column B?

Column A	Column B
1. _d_ Milk, orange juice, bread, toothpaste	**a.** casual conversation
2. _c_ Despite the protracted and contentious debate in the houses of government, the legislation was passed by a large margin, enabling the majority party to claim victory.	**b.** line from a script
	c. textbook sentence
	d. shopping list
3. _a_ Hey, did you enjoy the movie last night?	
4. _b_ Terence (*whispering*): Did you hear that moan?	

Was it a challenge for you? What clues allowed you to match the text in column A with the genre in column B? Which, if any, of the text examples do you associate with academic language? Which would you most likely find in written school materials? Why did you make these choices? You may have an intuitive notion as to the answers to these questions, but you may not have stopped to consider what academic language is and how it differs from social language. Further, you may not have fully developed your own skills in explicitly teaching academic language to students in your classes, yet for them to be successful in school and beyond, they need you and your colleagues to do so.

Defining Academic Language

Simply put, academic language is a second language for all students. Young children use everyday language at home. They engage socially with family and friends. They have books read to them, they tell stories, they play games. They may take walks and ask questions about the flowers and birds they notice. Their parents may ask them basic comprehension questions or seek their appraisal of a movie. Adults may ask them to compare a new experience with a prior one. But these young learners do not enter Grades K or 1 classrooms using embedded clauses and nominalizations in their conversations, nor do they analyze text for an author's bias or write persuasive essays about subject area topics. They learn these ways of using language for specific purposes over time in school. And school is where children and young adults mostly use academic language.

Academic language involves the use of higher-level vocabulary, more complex sentence structures, and more sophisticated forms of expression than are generally found in everyday conversation. It is the type of language students need to discuss complex ideas, articulate a position, summarize material, and contrast points of view. Education researchers have offered various definitions of academic language,[1] and while there is no singular definition, there is consensus that academic language includes the application of reading, writing, listening, and speaking skills to knowledge of vocabulary, language structures, language functions, genres, discourse patterns, and strategic competencies that students need to be successful in school with spoken and written academic text. There is also agreement that academic language demands and linguistic elements vary, at least partially, by subject area. Academic language is used by teachers and students. It is interpretive, productive, and interactional. Proficiency in academic language enables students to understand new information in the manner it is conveyed to them (orally, visually, or in writing) and to demonstrate and apply their knowledge through classroom tasks and assessments.

Figure 1.1 is a useful illustration of the complexity of academic language and helps capture why it takes considerable time to learn.

Think of this graphic as a clock. If we begin at 1 o'clock and move to 4 o'clock we see the five components of reading that the National Reading Panel identified as critical for academic reading (NICHD, 2000). As schools augmented reading periods to provide explicit

[1] For examples see Anstrom et al., 2010; Bailey & Heritage, 2008; Chamot & O'Malley, 1994; Coxhead, 2000; Gersten, et al., 2007; Gibbons, 2003; Goldenberg, 2008; Halliday, 1994; Scarcella, 2003; Schleppegrell, 2004; Short & Fitzsimmons, 2007; Snow & Uccelli, 2009; Zwiers, 2008.

Figure 1.1 **Elements of Academic Language and Literacy**

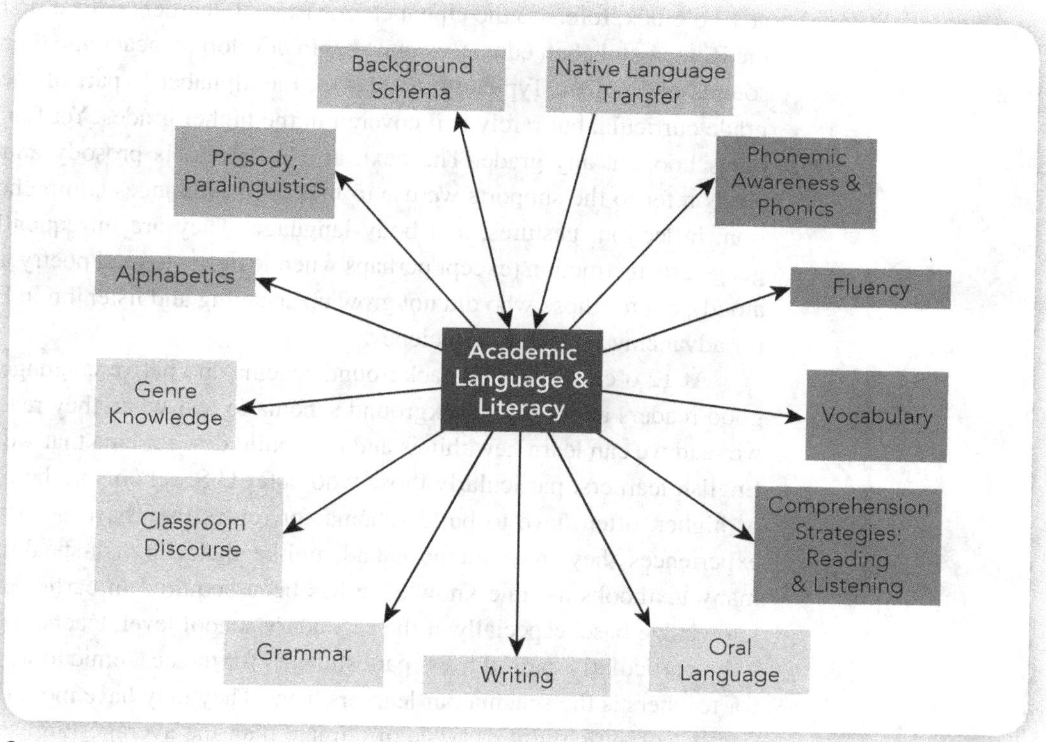

Source: D. Short, 2012

instruction in these five areas, ESL educators pointed out that English learners need more than basic reading skills to be successful in school (Saunders & Goldenberg, 2010). At the very least, additional instruction in the other language domains, namely listening, speaking, and writing, are necessary (see 4 o'clock to 6 o'clock). Unlike native English speakers who enter the primary grades with oral English skills, most English learners start with no or few skills in all the domains. In the diagram, listening comprehension is linked with reading comprehension because the cognitive strategies are similar. Instruction in these domains would be broken down into components as reading has been (e.g., pronouncing sounds and words, writing words and combining them into sentences, producing language functions for different purposes).

Language learning does not stop there, however. Educators of English learners also teach grammar to their students, sometimes embedded in writing instruction and sometimes in targeted mini-lessons on discrete points. They must teach the interaction patterns of classroom discourse, which are critical for active participation in academic settings. These patterns include turn-taking, building on others' ideas, and expressing agreement or disagreement with something a classmate has said or written. Teaching English learners to make meaning from different genres is needed too, and has been part of content-based English as a second language (ESL) and sheltered/SIOP instruction (Friend, Most, & McCrary, 2009; Short, 2013; Vogt, Echevarria & Short, 2010). These aspects of academic language and literacy are found at 7 o'clock through 9 o'clock. What is noteworthy is that reading, writing, listening, speaking, vocabulary, grammar, and genre knowledge are now part of the Common Core State Standards for English language arts (NGA, 2010a). In 44 states (at the time of this writing), English learners will be tested on these standards along with their English-speaking peers.

The remaining four items have some unique application to English learners. The first, at 10 o'clock, refers to the alphabet. For English learners whose first language does not use the Roman alphabet, educators must begin developing academic literacy with the letters and sounds of English. Typically in schools, the alphabet is part of the kindergarten and first grade curricula, but rarely is it covered in the higher grades. Yet English learners may enter our schools at any grade. The next, at 11 o'clock, is prosody and paralinguistics. These terms refer to the supports we use to make our utterances comprehensible, such as intonation, inflection, gestures, and body language. They are infrequently part of English language arts instruction (except perhaps when learning to read poetry and Shakespeare's plays aloud), but for those who did not grow up speaking and listening in English, they are critical for advancing language proficiency.

At 12 o'clock we find background schema and native language transfer. We know that good readers apply their background schema to text when they read. We also know that as we read we can learn new things and thus build new schema that we can apply in the future. English learners, particularly those who enter U.S. schools at the upper elementary grades or higher, often have to build schema for topics they have not studied previously or for experiences they may not have had, unlike their English-speaking classmates. Because many textbooks assume knowledge has been acquired in earlier grades and build on that knowledge base, especially at the secondary school level, teachers of English learners have to be particularly careful to prepare students for the academic topics. Another consideration for teachers is the schema our learners have. They may have more experience with political conflict or agriculture or types of climate than the average English-speaking classmate; if so, this knowledge should be tapped by effective teachers to enrich the classroom discourse.

Native language transfer is the final item in our figure. If students have literacy in their native language, many skills and knowledge bases will transfer to learning academic language and literacy in English. In some cases, students have a native language with the same letters and similar sounds systems as English. This knowledge will transfer easily. If students know how to read and find the main idea in a passage in their native language, they do not need to relearn that cognitive process. Yes, they will need to learn the words and syntax of English, but not the steps for determining the main idea. Further, any knowledge that students have learned through oral interaction in their native language (e.g., with their parents) is knowledge that can be tapped for background schema (Lindholm-Leary & Genesee, 2010).

Social and Academic Language

Academic language represents the range of language used in academic settings, including elementary and secondary schools. Essential for success in school, it is more challenging to learn than social, or conversational, English, especially for students who are acquiring English as a new language. Many students require four to seven years of study, depending on individual and sociocultural factors, to become proficient in academic English and to be on par with their English-speaking peers (Collier, 1987; Cook, Boals, & Lundberg, 2011; Hakuta, Butler, & Witt, 2000; Lindholm-Leary & Borsato, 2006; Thomas & Collier, 2002). Social language is generally more concrete than abstract, and it is usually supported by contextual clues, such as gestures, facial expressions, body language, and sometimes visual aids (Cummins, 1979; 2000; Echevarria & Graves, 2015). Knowing conversational language assists students in learning academic language, but it is only a launching point. We must go further and explicitly teach English learners subject area vocabulary, complex sentence structures, and rhetorical forms not typically used in everyday situations (Goldenberg, 2008). Native English speakers need this instruction as well.

In the education field, we used to talk about a dichotomy between social language and academic language. Cummins (1981) articulated the two categories as BICS (basic interpersonal communicative skills) and CALP (cognitive academic language proficiency), and his theories revolutionized instruction for English learners. As the movement toward standards-based education spread in U.S. schools, beginning with the national standards for mathematics in 1989 (NCTM, 1989), attention to preparing English learners for success in the content classroom grew. That preparation necessarily required explicit instruction in academic language as used in the different subject areas, in addition to subject-specific conceptual knowledge. Old notions of teaching English as a second language as if it were a foreign language course were put aside.

Over time the practice of exiting students from language development programs based on oral language proficiency was also curtailed. The need to teach some content to students and to strengthen their academic literacy skills, particularly in reading and writing, became paramount and galvanized changes to language development programs. More recently, classroom teachers in elementary and secondary schools have been responsible for developing English learners' language proficiency rather than relegating the responsibility to specialists. In some states, classroom teachers are required to provide focused English language development for a specified amount of time each day, most of which focuses on academic language.

Social Language	Academic Language
Hi, class. Let's get started.	Today we will be studying potential and kinetic energy.
I didn't like the article.	In my opinion, the article was inaccurate. There is no evidence that Russian cosmonauts landed on the moon.
Railroad tracks are parallel.	Alternate interior angles formed when a transversal intersects parallel lines are congruent.

Three decades later, our view of social and academic language has shifted from a dichotomy to more of a continuum. Consider the interaction in a typical classroom. Aspects of social language are often present. Teachers and students use high-frequency words and simple sentence structures—and these are found in academic texts and used in academic tasks too. However, the information presented is typically more complex in school than outside the classroom, and it increases in difficulty as students move up the grades and the content topics become more specialized. The use of the forms and functions of social language (e.g., simple sentence and question structures, simple language functions such as expressing likes and dislikes) diminish while academic forms and functions (e.g., sentences with embedded clauses and abstract concepts, higher-order language functions such as analyzing and justifying) escalate.

Think about encoding, for example. Students learn to write a word and next a simple sentence; then they proceed to complex, compound, and complex-compound sentences. They learn to relate sentences and organize them into a paragraph, choosing one to be a topic sentence. They learn to connect paragraphs at a higher discourse level with a specific purpose, such as to narrate a story, compare historical events, or interpret results of an experiment. The development of the ideas being conveyed is increasingly complex.

Now think back to the exercise at the beginning of this chapter. A shopping list did not strike you as academic text. It was not seemingly related to an academic topic. It was a list of words, not a sentence. It had no subject or verb. A casual conversation did have subjects and verbs, but did not identify it as academic text either. So what are characteristics of academic language? How do we know it when we read it or hear it?

Characteristics of Academic Language

Although we do not have a single definition of academic language in our field, there is widespread agreement that academic language is both general and subject-specific. **General academic language** is cross-curricular; in other words, it is applicable across content areas, and includes process and function words.[2] The following are examples:

- Nouns and verbs that can be used in many contexts, such as *argument, effect, circumstances, comprehension, define, analyze, represent,* and *encounter*
- Verbs and phrases that indicate procedures, actions, and uses of language, such as *classify, summarize,* and *compare*
- Conjunctions and transition words, such as *however, although, while,* and *in conclusion* that link ideas and concepts
- Sentence structures, such as *if–then* statements, relative clauses, and passive voice
- Grammatical features, such as comparative and superlative forms of adjectives, adverbs of time and place, and the perfect verb tenses

Subject-specific academic language tends to be more relevant to one content area than another. Examples include:

- Vocabulary that is associated with individual subjects (e.g., *exponent, numerator,* and *parabola* in mathematics; *legislation, medieval,* and *republic* for social studies; *characterization, author's purpose,* and *adverb* for language arts; *xylem, density,* and *lysosome* for science)
- Polysemous words that have a particular meaning in one subject and a different meaning in another (e.g., x to the 2nd *power* in algebra, judicial *power* in government, solar *power* in physical science)
- Text structures that are more common to certain subject areas than others (although rarely exclusive), such as cause–effect in science and problem–solution in mathematics

In academic text, ideas and concepts are connected structurally—through embedded clauses and conjunctions, for example—and lexically—through synonyms, words related to the same concept, and referents. The discourse structure is determined by the purpose of the text (e.g., comparison, causation, persuasion) and typically includes words to signal that purpose.

The following list describes characteristics of academic language. Not all of these descriptors are likely to be present in any given text, and in fact some may seem contradictory, such as *authoritative* versus *uncertain*. But the presence or absence of one is due to the

---

[2] Chapter 4 discusses academic vocabulary in depth.

purpose of the discourse (Uccelli, 2012). Is the author stating an unequivocal fact (authoritative) or hedging (uncertain) because the idea being conveyed has not yet been proven? Both are found in academic text. The first part of the list is more syntactical, referring to word choices and sentence formations. The second part of the list refers to the tone and presentation of information conveyed in a sentence, paragraph, or larger piece of text.

Academic Syntax

- **Long noun phrases**—Academic text often has noun phrases with multiple modifiers (e.g., *greatest common multiple* in math; *random sampling technique* in science).

- **Abstract nouns**—Academic text uses many abstract nouns, referring to concepts that cannot be shown with a picture or gesture (e.g., *representative democracy; theme*).

- **Nominalizations**—A process is transformed into a thing and the agent of action disappears; in brief, a verb is transformed into a noun form (e.g., "The sun evaporates the water" becomes "*Evaporation* occurs.").

- **Polysemy**—Multiple-meaning words are present; the definition in one subject area or context is not the definition in another (e.g., *root, attraction, mole, dependent* in science; *square, power, rational* in math).

- **Lexical precision**—Words are carefully chosen for clear, exact meanings (e.g., *bay* or *inlet* instead of "body of water").

- **Lexical diversity**—Authors of academic text typically use synonyms, pronouns, and other referents to refer to concepts already mentioned; English learners may struggle to find the antecedents or may know one word but not its synonyms (e.g., *add, increase, increase by, plus, more*, and *and* all indicate addition).

- **Lexical density**—A high number of words that convey information (e.g., nouns, adjectives, adverbs, and verbs) are present in a sentence, compared to words used for grammatical purposes (e.g., pronouns, prepositions, conjunctions); this is also related to higher use of pronominal antecedents and synonyms rather than repetition of the same content word (e.g., The *study findings indicate* that *English learners are able to retain* and *produce vocabulary terms learned* through *thematic text better than those learned* in *unrelated sentences.*).

- **Embedded clauses**—Ideas are linked through independent and dependent clause structures rather than as a series of short, choppy sentences (e.g., relative clauses—An equilateral triangle, *which has three equal sides and three equal angles*, differs from an isosceles triangle.).

- **Logical connectors and transition markers**—Wide use of conjunctions (e.g., coordinating conjunctions like *and* and *but*, subordinating conjunctions like *because* and *although*) to link ideas in a sentence and use of transitional words and phrases (e.g., *next, finally, in addition, in contrast, prior to, for example*) to link ideas across sentences and paragraphs.

- **Passive voice**—The subject of the sentence receives the action of the verb rather than performs it; the verb is usually constructed with a form of *to be* plus the past participle. If the agent of the action is known, it may be marked with *by* (e.g., The legislation was passed by the state senators.) Passive voice is used sometimes to avoid responsibility or when the agent doing the action is unknown.

- **Reported speech**—Academic discourse often reports on what others have written or reported using reported speech formats (rather than direct quotes) that can be confusing to English learners. "'Did the star collapse?' asked the scientist" becomes "The scientist asked if the star had collapsed." Verb tenses, adverbs of time, pronouns, and sometimes sentence word order change when direct speech is converted to reported speech.

- **Logical or sequential structure**—Text follows a discourse structure suited to its academic purpose. For example, when making an argument, the text follows a logical progression of points supporting the claim, perhaps also refuting counterclaims; when recounting a series of events, the text structure is sequential or chronological.

- **Conciseness**—Academic text packs a lot of information into a sentence and much more into a paragraph by using some of the elements mentioned above (e.g., long noun phrases, embedded clauses), along with precise word choices and by reducing redundancy (e.g., use *same*, not *exact same*) and unnecessary words.

- **Oral variations on written text**—In certain subjects, like math and science, there may be multiple ways of expressing terms orally (e.g., $(2x + y)/x^2$ can be either "two x plus y over x squared" or "the sum of two x and y divided by the square of x").

Academic Tone

- **Authoritative**—The author states facts or claims and provides evidence, and may assert strong opinions; the text may be persuasive or conclusive.

- **Cautious**—The author presents a theory or acknowledges an opinion but expresses lack of certainty or evidence and may call for research or support.

- **Detached**—The author is dispassionate or outside the action or findings, and may be connected to the passive voice.

- **Formal**—Academic text typically stays away from colloquial expressions and lends gravity to the information being presented through word choice and sentence structure.

Presentation

- **Text layout**—Academic text typically has less white space on the page and smaller font sizes than text encountered in everyday settings.

- **Directional tracking**—We teach students to read from left to right, but in some cases, they need to track text in other directions. Students read from right to left (as when reading an integer number line or a chemical equation), from top to bottom or vice versa (as when reading tables and charts), diagonally (as when reading some graphs), and holistically and with detail analysis (as when reading diagrams and images).

Academic Language in the Common Core and Next Generation Standards

Proficiency in academic language encompasses decoding meaning—determining what a passage states, a question asks, or a task requires—and encoding meaning—expressing one's thoughts, orally and in writing, in ways that can be communicated to and understood by others. Academic language skills are built on a foundation of vocabulary, grammar, fluency, phonics, and oral discourse. The skills needed for students to be college and career ready, however, extend from this base to include analytical reading and writing, effective communication and interaction, critical thinking, and creativity. These skills represent goals of the new Common Core State Standards for English language arts and literacy (NGA, 2010a) and for mathematics (NGA, 2010b), and of the Next Generation Science Standards (NGSS Lead States, 2013). We also find these skills in the standards of states like Texas and Virginia that did not adopt the Common Core.

In examining these new standards we see evidence of direct attention to academic language development in all subject areas (van Lier & Walqui, 2012). As in Figure 1.1, the academic language of the standards moves far beyond the five components of reading (NICHD, 2000). The following are key areas:

- **Vocabulary**—We see the importance of vocabulary in all three standards documents (English language arts [ELA], mathematics, and science) as they emphasize the need for students to communicate clearly, craft arguments, explain solutions, and the like. These in turn require students to determine meanings of words, distinguish between general academic and subject-specific terms, choose words carefully for oral and written purposes, and interpret nuances of words.

- **Genre Variety**—The Common Core language arts standards recommend that students spend approximately half their time working with informational texts. This is a shift from traditional curricula that included mostly fiction and poetry. Multiple genres are mentioned for language arts and other content areas, such as short stories, science articles, historical documents (primary and secondary sources), poems, biographies, interviews, digital texts and media, and more. Students also are expected to compose text in a number of these genres as well.

- **Complex Text**—The language arts and literacy standards in particular call for students to spend time working with complex text and to respond to comprehension questions based on the texts being read (Calkins, Ehrenworth, & Lehman, 2012; CCSS, 2010). However, it is important to remember that when working with English learners, any text beyond their reading level is complex for them. For instance, a text written at a Grade 4 reading level is likely to be complex for beginning-level English learners in that grade or any higher one, given their limited proficiency. Therefore, a complex text being analyzed by beginning-level students does not have to be a text written at the grade-level of their native-speaking peers; it may be at a lower reading level. As students advance in English proficiency, the texts they read should progress in complexity until they can read grade-level texts.

  The new standards also press teachers working with complex texts to move students beyond recalling basic information about what they have just read or explaining how a text made them feel. Instead, students must be encouraged to think critically—analyzing points of view, making inferences, synthesizing information, and connecting concepts across texts. Yet, being able to articulate their ideas along with these higher-order thinking processes requires significant academic language skill.

- **Listening and Speaking Targets**—Including listening and speaking standards in the Common Core is beneficial for English learners because research has shown that developing the four language skills—reading, writing, listening, and speaking—together is more effective for language acquisition than learning the skills in isolation (August & Shanahan, 2006; Carlo et al., 2004; Lesaux, Crosson, Keiffer & Pierce, 2010; Perez, 1981). Our students need to learn language functions and academic discourse patterns in order to participate in high levels of academic classroom talk, such as evaluating a historical perspective or presenting evidence for a scientific claim.

Effective communication involves the ability to use precise words, plan for a specific audience, and respond to the feedback in a conversation. If someone does not understand an utterance, then the speaker must rephrase or provide an example or find another way to make the message clear. If the listener has a follow-up question, the speaker must think about a response and then provide it.

- **Argumentation and Text-Based Evidence**—One particular language function that is called out in the language arts and literacy standards is argumentation. Students are expected to learn how to craft an argument and cite evidence for their ideas or opinions, both orally and in writing. The evidence may derive from a text or texts they have read, research they have done, an experiment they have conducted, or a video they have viewed. What constitutes evidence may vary by discipline. This argumentation function conceptually includes justification and persuasion and is applicable to all subject areas. The mathematics standards, for instance, ask students to use math language to solve and explain solutions to mathematical problems. The science standards require students to use reasoning to critique arguments and perspectives based on evidence that has been provided.

- **Critical Thinking and Creativity**—Critical thinking and creative activities may not seem language dependent at first glance. After all, they describe processes that take place in one's brain. But in practice, and in the spirit of college and career readiness, they require us to apply our knowledge. Although they can be accomplished non-verbally, the results must be expressed orally or in writing. Students generally need to listen and participate in academic talk in order to discuss their critical reasoning. Open-ended, higher-order questions and tasks by their very nature require more language knowledge to understand the intent of the question and to produce a response that communicates complex reasoning and describes abstract concepts.

Knowing these key areas of academic language in the new standards can help teachers prepare lessons that integrate appropriate language development with literacy and content area instruction. Teachers then can better tailor their lesson tasks to the language needs of the subjects, topics, and skills being taught.

Using Academic Language to Meet Standards

Let's examine some sample standards for their embedded academic language demands. One of the Anchor Standards for Reading in the Common Core language arts and literacy document for Grades K–12 is

- *Determine central ideas or themes of a text and analyze their development, and summarize the key supporting details and ideas.*

In order to accomplish this, students have to engage with text several ways:

1. Read the text (use knowledge of vocabulary, phonics, sentence structure).
2. Determine what the text is about and what key idea or theme it conveys (comprehend, infer, generalize, determine author's purpose).
3. Track the development of the idea or theme in the text (sequence, analyze).
4. Summarize the details and ideas that support the main idea or theme (distinguish between supporting details and main ideas, identify essential information, present

information succinctly, remove extraneous information, choose words carefully, form summary sentences).

As you can see, a seemingly straightforward standard has multiple components, each of which requires a high level of language knowledge and use. The next example shows the language demands of math processes in one of the Common Core Math Standards for Grade 3:

- *Students develop an understanding of fractions, beginning with unit fractions. Students view fractions in general as being built out of unit fractions, and they use fractions along with visual fraction models to represent parts of a whole. Students understand that the size of a fractional part is relative to the size of the whole. For example, 1/2 of the paint in a small bucket could be less paint than 1/3 of the paint in a larger bucket, but 1/3 of a ribbon is longer than 1/5 of the same ribbon because when the ribbon is divided into 3 equal parts, the parts are longer than when the ribbon is divided into 5 equal parts. Students are able to use fractions to represent numbers equal to, less than, and greater than one. They solve problems that involve comparing fractions by using visual fraction models and strategies based on noticing equal numerators or denominators.*

While there is clearly a focus on mathematical understanding of fractions and visual representations, expressing such understanding will require students to use math language in ways such as the following:

1. Make comparisons, orally or in writing (use comparative adjectives and forms: *longer than, less than*; use symbols: $<, =, >$).
2. Use math vocabulary accurately (e.g., *fraction, numerator, denominator, equal*).
3. Express math reasoning (give examples, express causation: *if–then, because*).

Similarly we find use of academic language necessary for meeting the performance expectations of the Next Generation Science Standards. The example below is for high school life science, focusing on ecosystems:

- *Evaluate the claims, evidence, and reasoning that the complex interactions in ecosystems maintain relatively consistent numbers and types of organisms in stable conditions, but changing conditions may result in a new ecosystem.*

In order to demonstrate their understanding of the standard, students will:

1. Make comparisons and contrasts (use comparative adjectives and forms, use conjunctions to express relationships between ideas).
2. Weigh points in an argument (read or listen to claims and others' reasoning, interpret new information and compare to known information).
3. Synthesize information and construct an argument in favor of or opposed to one given (sort and consolidate information gathered through reading or listening, express agreement or disagreement, state evidence or counterclaims).

It's your turn. Examine one of your state standards for the embedded academic language demands. Notice if the standard refers to language functions and/or skills.

This brief look at three standards shows us that all teachers, not just ESL teachers, will need to focus on academic language in their content areas so the students can meet these rigorous goals.

What Teachers Need to Know about Teaching Academic Language to English Learners

Some excellent, informative books and articles explain second language acquisition principles and the role of language in academic settings; others offer teachers guidance about teaching language to linguistically and culturally diverse students at school.[3] We will not attempt to summarize all the important information in these works here, but will highlight certain key points for teachers to keep in mind (see Figure 1.2).

First, we should re-emphasize that academic language is a second language for all. Students learn to interact with academic writing and participate in academic conversations in school. Teachers build on the everyday language students bring to school to develop their facility with academic language.

Second, we must remember that English learners have to do double the work in schools: they must learn English *and* learn content, but they are not given double the time (Short & Fitzsimmons, 2007). With the exception of a one-year's grace period for language arts assessments, English learners are evaluated with the same tests as their native English-speaking classmates, no matter what their English proficiency level is. That is why it is imperative for all teachers to help English learners both acquire English and learn content. Content-area/classroom teachers must integrate academic language and literacy into their lessons and ESL/ELD teachers must add content topics to their language classes. As students improve their academic English skills, they also will increase their content area achievement scores (Cook, Boals, & Lundberg, 2011). In brief, the teachers have to double up too, just like the students, to achieve success in school.

Third, it is important to note that English learners come to school with assets that will support their development of academic language proficiency. These assets are related to language practices in the home. For example, children learn to make guesses and predictions at home. In school they learn to call these notions *estimates, hypotheses,* or *theories* depending on the subject area and context. All can act as precursors to academic language

Figure 1.2   Key Points to Remember When Teaching Academic Language to English Learners

1. Academic language is a second language for all learners in school.
2. English learners must do double the work: learn English while they learn content.
3. English learners bring many assets to the classroom that can support academic language development.
4. Individual factors affect the rate and degree of academic language development.
5. It takes time to learn academic English, and English learners are often tested in English before they are proficient.
6. Students need opportunities to learn both English and content through quality programs and instruction.
7. There is no one-size-fits-all solution.

---

[3] See, for example, Adger, Snow & Christian, 2002; August & Shanahan, 2008; California Department of Education, 2010; Cloud, Genesee & Hamayan, 2009; Genesee, Lindholm-Leary, Saunders, & Christian, 2006; Gersten et al., 2007; Goldenberg, 2008; Seedhouse, Walsh, & Jenks, 2010.

development. Teachers need to be aware of the language and literacy skills the students have and use outside of school.

These assets include:

- **Native language and literacy knowledge**—As mentioned earlier, many aspects of the native language learned at home can apply or transfer to learning academic English (August & Shanahan, 2006; Genesee et al., 2006; Guglielmi, 2008; Restrepo & Gray, 2007). These include phonemic awareness and phonics, vocabulary cognates, knowledge of affixes and roots, and reading/listening comprehension strategies. In addition, the knowledge students have learned through their native language is a resource to be tapped. Further, students who have learned a second language already and are adding English as a third or fourth language will generally acquire English more easily.

- **Out-of-school literacies**—Students learn to use literacy outside of school, sometimes for family purposes (e.g., making a shopping list, reading a bill, calling for a doctor's appointment) and sometimes for personal reasons (e.g., listening to music, sending texts, reading websites). Students learn to navigate the Internet and social media. They are sometimes more media savvy than their teachers. These practices help them understand that literacy is used for different purposes and is found in different formats (Alvermann & Moore, 2011; Skerrett & Bomer, 2011; Xu, 2008).

- **Language brokering**—School-aged English learners often assume the role of language broker in families where the adults do not speak English or are less proficient in it (Cline, Crafter, O'Dell, & de Abreu, 2011; Halgunseth, 2003). Students learn to engage with others using English, experiencing different interaction patterns, and being responsive to others' utterances. Notions of turn-taking, asking for clarification, and paraphrasing, for example, are practiced, as may be interpreting and translating, when young learners fill this role.

- **Sociolinguistic and sociocultural practices**—In their homes and cultures, students learn norms for using their native language. These norms involve a range of behaviors and expectations, such as the degree of formality to use when addressing others, the length of pauses between sentences or utterances, eye contact, word choice, and more. Sometimes these norms are similar to language use expectations in U.S. classrooms, and sometimes they are not. If not, students benefit when teachers explain the classroom culture and teach students how to participate (Tharp & Gallimore, 1988).

- **Codeswitching**—It is natural for proficient bilinguals to codeswitch; and, contrary to common belief, codeswitching is not a sign of semi-literacy or of secrecy (Nilep, 2006). Codeswitching, that is, switching between two languages during a single conversation, can be a strategic resource. Languages often have words that are more precise than their translation in a different language. For example, in Spanish the term *ganas* means "desire" or "wish," but the English translation of the word does not quite capture its essence. Someone might say, "I'm going to get some coffee. I've got *ganas* for a cappuccino."

Fourth, individual factors affect the rate and degree of academic language development. Below we explain a few of these—prior schooling, motivation, and mobility. Additional ones include personality, learning style, social identity, and age.

- **Prior schooling**—Students with strong academic backgrounds in their native language typically develop academic language skills in English more readily than those who have had limited formal schooling (Riches & Genesee, 2006). Those who developed native language academic literacy have relevant cognitive strategies and higher-order thinking skills and have had significant practice using academic language. Students who have not developed literacy in their native language will need to develop it for the first time in the new, unfamiliar language.

- **Motivation**—Most English learners in U.S. schools are eager to learn English. They exhibit both intrinsic and extrinsic motivation. But for some, years of poor instruction or lack of progress in their language development can diminish their drive to become proficient. For these students, "more of the same" is rarely successful. They need different interventions that build on their strengths and the knowledge they already have and that target underdeveloped aspects of their academic literacy.

- **Mobility**—Students in families that move frequently experience educational interruptions that can interfere with academic language development (Glick & White, 2004). With the advent of new standards, students who move may find that their new school has a similar curriculum for English language arts, mathematics, and/or science, and so may not duplicate or skip content in those subjects, but the other subjects' and the English language development curricula could be quite different. Further, the socio-emotional stress involved with moving can hinder students' academic development.

> Think of two English learners in your class or school. What are some individual factors that may affect the rate at which they acquire academic English?

Fifth, we should recognize it takes time to learn academic English and schools need common-sense policies about accountability measures. Most English learners are tested in English before they are proficient in English. As a result, on state assessments, the average scores of English learners reveal an achievement gap when compared with those of native English speakers. That gap should be expected and acknowledged *pro forma* in the public reporting of scores. Teachers and schools should not be penalized if students designated as English learners do not reach proficient levels on these tests, because by definition they are not yet proficient.

Districts would benefit from disaggregating test scores to look at how the exited English learners perform. They should not have an achievement gap when their scores are compared with those of native speakers if they are given time to develop academic English proficiency in their programs and are exited/redesignated with criteria that measure their ability to be successful in mainstream classes. New York City and the states of New Jersey, Washington, and California have done these types of analyses and have found that former English learners outperformed students as a whole on state tests, exit exams, and graduation rates (DeLeeuw, 2008; New York City Department of Education, 2004; State of New Jersey Department of Education, 2006; Sullivan et al., 2005).

Sixth, it is critical that students be offered opportunities to learn English and content through quality programs and instruction. Quality indicators include:

- Language support programs of three years' or more duration that include sheltered content classes and English language development or English as a second language classes.

- Teachers knowledgeable about the language of their subject area and trained in techniques that integrate language and content development.

- Teachers well informed about sociocultural practices who are able to co-construct a classroom environment that promotes respect, learning, and interaction among all students.

- Classroom settings that are conducive to interaction—no cemetery headstone set-ups where all the desks are in a row facing forward; desks should be clustered.

- Instructional materials that include resources in English and native languages, representing multiple genres and texts at and above the students' reading levels.

- Lessons that engage students by tapping their interests and knowledge, building background schema, offering choices about activities and partners, and providing scaffolds to support their success in learning new material and accomplishing assigned tasks.

Finally, we must remember that there is no one-size-fits-all solution. For example, non-English speaking students with limited formal schooling and no native language literacy may need to begin instruction in a newcomer class, while those who have had schooling and are literate may begin with the equivalent of an ESL 1 course. This caveat is especially important if a student who has been in the program for two years or more is not making expected progress. We need to examine these situations on a case-by-case basis. Questions we might pursue are:

- Which skills has the student acquired and which are lagging behind expectations?

- Are conditions outside school interfering with the learning process?

- Does the student have a learning disability?

- Does the student suffer from test anxiety?

These students would benefit from an intervention targeted to their specific needs to ensure they continue to make progress toward full proficiency in academic English.

Addressing Academic Language with the SIOP Model

Standards such as the Common Core and Next Generation tell teachers what students need to learn and do as a result of instruction. They do not, however, tell teachers how to teach. The Sheltered Instruction Observation Protocol Model, better known as the SIOP Model (Echevarría, Vogt & Short, 2013), shows teachers how to plan and deliver effective standards-based lessons. As discussed above, the new standards embed a considerable amount of academic language in both their individual explanations and their expected student performances. The SIOP Model can help teachers and students meet those language demands. It offers a pedagogical approach for teaching academic language development at the same time content is taught, in a manner that is comprehensible to English learners. The SIOP Model has been tested empirically in several research studies over fifteen years and has been shown to be effective in improving students' academic English skills (Batt, 2010; Echevarria, Richards-Tutor, Canges, & Francis, 2011; Echevarria, Short & Powers, 2006; McIntyre, et al., 2010; Short, Echevarria, & Richards-Tutor, 2011; Short, Fidelman, & Louguit, 2012). A copy of the SIOP Model protocol listing its 30 features is found in Appendix A.

Well-implemented SIOP instruction incorporates all four language skills—reading, writing, listening, and speaking—in lessons across the content areas. Teachers using this model purposefully plan scaffolding, building background, and vocabulary activities to make lessons accessible to English learners. Scaffolding provides support for students as they learn to do a task independently. For example, scaffolds may help students understand procedures (e.g., watch the teacher model a task step by step), process the new material being taught (e.g., add notes to a partially completed outline while reading a section of the textbook), or practice how to orally describe a diagram (e.g., use sentence starters: *The illustration on the left shows . . . , The arrow indicates . . .*). The goal is to reduce and eventually remove scaffolds as students gain academic language proficiency.

Teachers using the SIOP Model also develop their students' background knowledge (e.g., through multimedia and hands-on experiences) in order to facilitate their reading comprehension skills and to set them up for adding content information to their knowledge base. By pre-teaching key vocabulary and giving students multiple opportunities to use the new words (e.g., with vocabulary routines, games, and graphics), teachers build students' conceptual knowledge. Teachers also help students learn strategies to determine the meanings of unknown words.

Several features of the SIOP Model promote the type of oral interaction called for in the Common Core and Next Generation standards. SIOP teachers design lessons that build oral discourse skills and use oral language to support and strengthen reading and writing. Teachers include techniques that require student–student communication, such as collaborative group activities, pair work, debate teams, literature circles, author's chair, and role-play. They may assign projects that ask students to create something new, such as a cover for a literary magazine or a summary of an article related to a topic being studied in science. There are also opportunities to enhance oral presentation skills, for instance, by presenting information about a topic to the class.

The rest of this book focuses on ways that teachers can consciously and effectively incorporate academic language teaching into their daily lessons. In particular, we advocate implementing the SIOP Model of instruction to make academic material comprehensible and to develop students' academic language skills. The principles and techniques are applicable not only to English learners but also to other students who are not proficient in using academic English. If you are not familiar with the basic SIOP Model framework, we suggest you read one of the main texts first. *Making Content Comprehensible for English Learners: The SIOP Model* (Echevarria, Vogt & Short, 2013) explains the model with examples for Grades K through 12, while *Making Content Comprehensible for Elementary English Learners: The SIOP Model* (Echevarria, Vogt & Short, 2014a) and *Making Content Comprehensible for Secondary English Learners: The SIOP Model* (Echevarria, Vogt & Short, 2014b), as their names suggest, target the information to Grades K–6 and Grades 6–12, respectively. For those serving our youngest learners, *Using the SIOP Model with Pre-K and Kindergarten English Learners* (Echevarria, Short, & Peterson, 2012) may be most appropriate.

Summary

Remember that language is the key to learning. Language reflects how we think—how we acquire, process, remember, and connect information. Language offers us an important way to articulate and extend our ideas (Vygotsky, 1978). Using academic language, we can describe what is in our environment or visualize a different setting. We can hypothesize, research, and draw conclusions about science phenomena. We can justify a solution to a math problem or compare two novels on similar themes with a peer. Language allows us to broaden our knowledge base and make sense of our experiences.

Academic language proficiency is the ability to use academic language for various purposes and with different audiences in ways that are valued in individual subject-area

disciplines. When students are proficient in academic language, they can use their knowledge of language:

- to learn new information,
- to demonstrate knowledge of information,
- to apply information,
- to be creative and form opinions,
- to perform academic tasks.

Such proficiency involves the application of cognitive and metacognitive strategies, background schema (including knowledge learned through another language), and higher-order
thinking skills.

We need to help English learners and other students who struggle with academic literacy to develop their academic language skills and become facile using academic language
for multiple purposes and with a variety of audiences. We need to set up optimal learning
conditions in our classes where students have many practice opportunities for using academic language and strong models of appropriate and interesting uses of it. We hope that
the following chapters guide you in designing and delivering lessons that engage students in
learning and using academic language effectively.

Questions for Reflection

1. It is well established that there is a difference between language used for social
   purposes and academic language. Explain the distinction between the two. In what
   ways are social and academic language interrelated, and how are both used in the
   classroom?

2. Select at least five of the characteristics of academic language listed in the chapter and
   describe each one in your own words. Then, using a student textbook, find an example
   of each of the characteristics you selected.

3. How does understanding the characteristics of academic language assist you in lesson
   planning? What might you do differently in your lessons after having read this chapter?

4. Discussions about the education of English learners often focus on what skills they
   have yet to acquire. However, English learners possess a number of assets that support
   and may even accelerate their acquisition of academic language. What are some of
   those assets? How might you tap into students' assets and incorporate them in
   lessons?

2

Maximizing Language Development in Lessons

Fotolia

In this chapter you will

Content Objectives:

- Identify the eight components of the SIOP Model
- Explain three types of learning strategies that support academic language development

Language Objectives:

- Summarize the features of SIOP's components that focus on language development
- Modify lesson plans to create more language learning opportunities

In our work with elementary and secondary teachers, we have found that many do not recognize the teachable language moments in their lessons. Those who have trained as grade-level or subject-area teachers often notice the content learning that takes place among their students and recognize moments when students have an "aha" reaction related to a key concept, but they are less cognizant of the "aha" language moments and less prepared to elicit or take advantage of them.

ACTIVITY

Take a guess. How many of the 30 features in the SIOP Model focus on language development? Now look at the SIOP Protocol in Appendix A. Confirm or correct your guess. Which features focus on language?

When we developed the SIOP Model as an approach for teaching English learners, our goal was to create a framework that shows teachers how to integrate language and content instruction and identifies key elements that should be included in every lesson delivered to students learning content through a new language. In looking at the protocol now, almost two decades later, we are pleased that with the growing awareness of the role of academic language in schools—for all students—16 of the 30 SIOP features focus on language development (see Figure 2.1). We didn't intentionally plan a fairly even distribution of language features, but through the early years of research and refinement, that is how it turned out. And how valuable is the result, to demonstrate the balance that is needed in every lesson!

Figure 2.1 Opportunities to Develop Academic Language in the SIOP Model

Lesson Preparation

- In Feature 2, teachers must define clear language objectives in their lesson plans, post the objectives for students to read, and review them orally with students.
- In Feature 6, teachers are encouraged to plan meaningful activities that incorporate language and content practice opportunities.

Building Background

- Feature 9 emphasizes vocabulary that needs to be introduced to students and practiced during the lessons.

Comprehensible Input

- Teacher speech is the focus of Feature 10. The words, idioms, and syntax that teachers use can contribute to student comprehension and can strengthen students' listening skills if carefully planned, but they can also add to students' confusion if the speech is far above their ability to understand.

Strategies

- Feature 13 addresses explicit teaching of learning strategies to students; these include vocabulary strategies, reading comprehension strategies, and other language learning strategies such as using native language resources, self-monitoring, and rehearsing.
- The scaffolding emphasis of Feature 14 reminds teachers to support English learners' language use, but as the students advance in proficiency, teachers need to remove some of the supports so students can use academic language independently.
- Although the words of Feature 15 focus on higher-order *thinking*, the practical application involves sophisticated language knowledge and use. Even if students think critically in their first language, to articulate their understandings, they need to use academic language.

Interaction

- Feature 16 focuses on increasing student-to-student interaction in a structural way and also calls for elaborated speech on the part of the students. Thus the English learners have to provide more than one- or two-word responses and work on framing their responses using appropriate academic terms and phrasings.
- The grouping configurations teachers design as part of Feature 17 should connect to the language objectives and encourage student language practice.
- Feature 19 enables teachers and students to make use of students' native language for clarification. The first language thus becomes a resource for learning the meanings of new academic terms and for language transfer opportunities (depending on the native language) such as using cognates, decoding words, and forming sentences.

Practice & Application

- Features 21 and 22 remind teachers to include activities that give students opportunities to practice and apply all skills and knowledge across the four language domains.

Lesson Delivery

- This component holds the teacher accountable during the lesson, and Feature 24 specifically addresses whether the teacher helped the students meet the language objective(s) of the lesson through the presentation and activities.

(Continued)

Saiscultural Competency - know the

Figure 2.1   Opportunities to Develop Academic Language in the SIOP Model *(Continued)*

Review & Assessment

- Teachers are asked to review the key vocabulary of the lesson in Feature 27. This helps English learners remember the key words and related concepts each day.
- Feature 29 calls on teachers to offer feedback to students on their academic language use. This provides the opportunity for teachers to improve student academic language skills in context, whether it be related to pronunciation, sentence structure, or word choice.
- Assessing student learning informally is an important element of lesson design. Feature 30 reminds teachers to assess student language use throughout the lesson, and not just focus on content comprehension.

The purpose of this chapter is to help teachers anticipate when and where language learning can and should take place in SIOP lessons. Specifically, we will walk through the SIOP components and identify the features where academic language development is paramount and explain how to maximize language learning in the lessons.

Lesson Preparation

Lesson preparation is one of the most important aspects of teaching and also the most neglected. Teachers generally map out what they are going to teach for a given lesson, but in order to advance student learning and language development, it is critical that teachers plan carefully. As you begin considering the academic language you teach in every lesson more closely, the planning will become easier and go more quickly. But initially it will take time to implement the lesson planning we advocate for meeting the needs of both your English learners and other students who would benefit from more attention to academic literacy.

The lesson preparation component has two features directly connected to academic language learning, Feature 2 and Feature 6. Feature 2 allows teachers to explicitly plan for a language goal in their lessons and Feature 6 makes sure the lesson has practice activities to give the students an opportunity to make progress in developing their academic language knowledge.

Lesson Preparation

2. Language objectives clearly defined, displayed, and reviewed with students.
6. Meaningful activities that integrate lesson concepts with language practice opportunities for reading, writing, listening, and/or speaking.

SIOP® Feature #2

Language Objectives Defined

When we first introduced the idea of having language objectives in every lesson in the 1990s, many content teachers did not think of their lessons as having the dual purpose of teaching both the lesson's content and the language required for understanding that content. Currently, however, widespread understanding of the importance of language in learning has led many instructional approaches and materials to highlight both content and language objectives.

observed in practicum

In Feature 2, teachers are told to define clear language objectives for their lessons, post written objectives for students to read, and review them orally with the class. Further, and most importantly, they are to plan instructionally to address the objectives and give students an opportunity to work toward mastering them.

Some favorite ways that teachers have shared with us for engaging students in thinking about the objectives include the following:

- Student pairs discuss what they think they will learn based on the written objectives.
- Students focus on the verbs in the objectives to determine what they will be doing and learning.
- Students select one objective that may be meaningful to them that day and reflect on how well they met it at the end of the lesson.
- Students decide which objective may be most challenging and then revisit their progress in meeting it at the end of the lesson.

Based on our years of work with teachers and our research with the SIOP Model, we suggest four categories for language objectives (LOs) that teachers can draw from in order to develop LOs for their lessons (Echevarria, Vogt & Short, 2013). These categories are:

- **Academic vocabulary:** Key concepts (*democracy, characterization*), subject-specific or technical terms (*mitosis, isosceles triangle*), general academic terms (*result, involve*), function words (*compare, persuade*), logical connectors and transition words (*finally, unless, in addition*), and word parts (prefixes, suffixes, roots)
- **Language functions and skills:** Language as used in the lesson while they speak, read, write, or listen to information related to the lesson topic (e.g., students read to find evidence supporting a claim in the text, students make predictions, students draft a laboratory report)
- **Language structures and grammar:** Structures in the spoken and written discourse of the lesson (e.g., students must interpret passive voice or embedded clauses in text)
- **Language learning strategies:** Mental strategies that students use to make sense of oral and written text, to organize information, to monitor language production, and to apply skills to language tasks

Teachers are comfortable teaching vocabulary because they regularly do so and many key terms are highlighted in their textbooks. While vocabulary may be the "low-hanging fruit," it is not the sole area for language development since vocabulary acquisition alone will not fully develop students' ability to use language in ways that are required in school and in careers. We encourage teachers to use the following process to determine language objectives:

1. Identify the language demands of the standards-based lesson concepts or tasks you plan to include in your lessons.
2. Determine which ones your students would benefit from explicit instruction on.
3. Write observable objectives that focus on those skills.
4. Design the lesson to ensure practice opportunities.

This selection process may be challenging for teachers who are not accustomed to thinking about the academic language of their content area. There is always a wide range of language objective possibilities—how can teachers winnow it down? And once an LO is chosen, how can they be sure to provide explicit instruction and practice activities for the students? The activity alone, such as reading four pages in a book, is not sufficient as a language objective. Instruction must be provided in, for example, how to read, or what to read for, or what to do with the information read. Possible corresponding objectives might instead be:

- Students will read aloud using appropriate intonation and inflection based on punctuation.
- Students will read a passage on magnetism to determine the main idea and supporting details.
- Students will read about parallelograms and orally compare two shapes with a partner.

Chapter 3 of this book focuses on the selection, writing, and delivering of language objectives in lesson plans.

SIOP® Feature #6

Meaningful Activities

Although the objectives establish the main language focus of each lesson, other opportunities for language development will be present. Feature 6 is a case in point. Content teachers are skillful at creating practice activities for students to deepen their understanding of subject area topics. Language teachers are likewise very able to design tasks for students to practice language goals. In order for lessons to be effective for all learners, we want both types of teachers to incorporate practice opportunities for content *and* language learning. The activities need to be relevant to the lesson concepts and should give students a chance to read, speak, listen, and write about the content topics—if not each day, then over the course of several days.

Meaningful activities are authentic and relevant. Unfortunately, English learners are often assigned activities that are not meaningful and are unrelated to the tasks given to the English-proficient students in their classes. Content standards that apply to students with English proficiency must also apply to English learners. However, it is in the planning process that teachers make decisions about scaffolding and other adjustments to instruction so that the intended activities supporting these standards are accessible to English learners. We hope never to observe another lesson like one we saw in our first SIOP research study. One of the comparison teachers (i.e., not SIOP-trained) had her 7th grade English learners coloring pictures of butterflies in science class, while the lesson for English speakers was focused on the life cycle of a caterpillar. Our English learners are students who can least afford to have time wasted with irrelevant, non-academic activities.

To help students participate in meaningful activities, teachers may have to pre-teach vocabulary words, give a jumpstart lesson that builds background, scaffold the procedures for a task, or provide sentence starters so students can express their thoughts. Carefully planned meaningful activities are also culturally responsive ones—with students' multiple perspectives welcomed and their cultural backgrounds respected. Students' native languages should also be used to help transfer skills or to clarify information. The activities overall should call on students to interact with text, task, and each other, using several of the four language domains within each activity.

Building Background

Two misconceptions surrounding the Common Core State Standards, particularly in English/language arts, are that students are required to spend an entire lesson reading the text and that teachers ought not to spend time building students' background knowledge and linking their experiences to the text. It is true that the CCSS emphasize the importance of exposure to grade-level text and call for more time spent with students engaged in reading. But background can be built and activated. Teachers are cautioned, though, not to waste instructional time on unfocused discussions that are tangential to the text.

In the Building Background component, Features 7 and 8 encourage language development indirectly, but that is not their main purpose. When we ask teachers to make links to the students' personal lives (Feature 7), there are often opportunities for oral language practice—to retell a song, poem, or legend they heard as a child, or recount an adventure related to the topic. English learners benefit from a discussion of previous learning (Feature 8) not only to reinforce the concepts but also to provide additional practice with academic English (e.g., using vocabulary or language structures they have been studying).

Building Background

9. Key vocabulary emphasized (e.g., introduced, written, repeated, and highlighted for students to see).

 ## SIOP® Feature #9

Vocabulary Emphasized

The main feature in the Building Background component that explicitly promotes academic language development is Feature 9, which is focused on vocabulary. We all know the importance of vocabulary learning. Simply put, the students who know the most words do the best in school. As one learns more and more words, one learns more about the concepts that the words are associated with. Deep conceptual knowledge is important for academic success. Having a wider vocabulary also means one generally knows more synonyms and related words, as well as multi-meaning words. This knowledge becomes strategic during assessments when knowing terms associated with the key words in the test question can help a student evaluate responses in multiple choice contexts or craft a constructed answer that is on point.

The Common Core English/language arts standards acknowledge the importance of this topic with a strand focused on vocabulary acquisition and use that is applicable from kindergarten through Grade 12. Students are expected to determine the meaning of new words and use strategies (e.g., examination of affixes or of context) to do so. They are also expected to apply knowledge of these words in their reading, writing, listening, and speaking activities.

Researchers recommend that students learn 2,000–3,000 words each year from 3rd grade on to be ready for college or a career at the end of high school (Graves, 2006). Typically a student learns 5–10 words per week in a particular subject. With only 36–40 weeks in a school year, that equals a range of 180–400 words per year per subject. If students learned 10 words per week in 5 subjects, we would reach 2,000 words per year, the minimum that research suggests. But does that really happen? And is it enough? Some researchers also indicate that students should have a reading vocabulary of 50,000 words by the end of 12th grade in order to be prepared for college or a technical school. After 12 years of schooling, at 2,000 words per year, students would reach 24,000 words.

The twist is that when researchers count a "word," they are actually counting a word family, that is, a word and all of its forms and fixed expressions. So, the word *go* counts as one word even though its forms encompass *go, went, gone, going,* and phrasal verbs like *go on, go over,* and more. It is no surprise that researchers urge teachers to ramp up the number of words they teach, so students can learn more words and have a better chance at academic success. In truth, though, students will need to learn words on their own as well, and so we need to give them tools to facilitate the process.

As mentioned above, academic vocabulary can be a focus for a lesson's language objective. But even if it is not the objective of the day, it needs to be part of every lesson. We know students need multiple exposures to words—12–15 by some counts—that go beyond seeing the words printed on a flash card that number of times. Students need to learn what the words mean, how they can be used (e.g., part of speech, use in sentences), and what they sound like spoken aloud. Students need to say the word, read text with the words, write the words in different contexts, and listen to others use the words. Over time, 12–15 engagements with the words will help students learn them and make them part of their reading and speaking repertoire.

In Chapter 4 we explore ways to promote academic vocabulary development.

Comprehensible Input

Because English learners are doing double the work every day, it is important for teachers to make the new information being taught through the new language as accessible as possible. Accomplished teachers adjust their rate of speech, word choice, and sentence structure complexity according to the proficiency levels of the students. They make content comprehensible through content-ESL techniques and also explain academic tasks clearly, both orally and in writing, providing models and examples wherever possible.

Comprehensible Input

10. Speech appropriate for students' proficiency level (e.g., slower rate, enunciation, and simple sentence structure for beginners).

SIOP® Feature #10

Appropriate Teacher Speech

The CCSS and other state standards ask for a more sophisticated level of language use, so teachers need to be very aware of their enunciation, rate of speech, vocabulary usage, and oral delivery during lessons. How a teacher modulates his or her speech in accordance with the proficiency levels and comprehension of the students is critical to engaging students in the lesson. We encourage teachers to consider their utterances carefully. With newcomers and beginners, they want to speak more slowly but with natural language patterns and clear articulation. They should not pause between each word, but pause at phrase and clause breakpoints. They should pronounce the words distinctly. They should choose words carefully—simple and familiar terms, few synonyms, and few idioms. The sentences also should be shorter and simpler for this student group. Teachers can enhance their speech with gestures and movements to give clues to meaning. Adding intonation and expression can also help students understand.

Teachers should not, however, rely on simplified speech with all students. As students reach the intermediate and advanced levels of English, teacher speech should become more sophisticated. When students are ready to make the transition out of the English language program and into the mainstream program, they should have experienced their teachers talking to them as the teachers talk to native English speakers. The SIOP Model asks teachers to be cognizant of their students' abilities and to push them forward with oral input that is slightly beyond their comfort zone.

In classes with students of mixed proficiency levels, the teacher may direct whole class instruction at the mid-range, but individual comments and questions can be phrased for each student's level. Teachers can also plan in advance a differentiated series of questions to pose. This is particularly valuable when trying to provide opportunities for all students to respond to higher-order questions. Teachers can simplify word choice and structure in questions for newcomers and beginners but still pose questions that require critical analysis or evaluation. Finally, in mixed classes, teachers need to make sure they give enough wait time to less proficient students.

What teachers choose to say and when can increase comprehensibility for students. Repetition, for instance, helps students learn words and phrases. Paraphrasing and restating can help students understand another's speech. While reading aloud, teachers can pause and define words or explain a difficult piece of text. In addition, teachers use their questions to prompt students to use academic language and extend their ideas.

Teachers are valuable language models to students. As students begin to learn English and later become more proficient, they tend to emulate their teachers' speech. The Common Core State Standards call for students to meet benchmarks for listening and speaking. Modeling academic language phrasings—whether it is how to link a character's traits to his or her actions, how to state a comparison between two classes of animals, or how to make a counterclaim—is one way that teachers can help students meet these standards.

Strategies

The long-term goal of this component is to equip students with the critical thinking skills and strategies they will need to be successful in school and beyond. Most professions require such skills and strategies, and school is an ideal venue to help students develop them. All three features of this component have a direct connection to academic language learning, because we need knowledge of academic language to process complex tasks and to articulate abstract reasoning.

Consider the following key processes in the reading standards of the Common Core English/Language Arts State Standards: *read closely, make logical inferences, cite specific evidence, support claims, analyze, summarize, interpret, assess,* and *evaluate.* Similar processes are found in the Common Core Mathematics Standards: *interpret, analyze, reason abstractly, construct, solve, apply and extend,* and *summarize.* When these become instructional tasks, they require students to use complex cognitive processes and strategic thinking while comprehending and using academic language to demonstrate competence.

Strategies

13. Ample opportunities provided for students to use learning strategies.

14. Scaffolding techniques consistently used assisting and supporting student understanding (e.g., think-alouds).

15. A variety of question types used including those that promote higher-order thinking skills (e.g., open-ended questions rather than questions with yes/no responses).

 SIOP® Feature #13

Explicit Teaching of Learning Strategies

Decades of research show the importance of having teachers explicitly teach learning strategies to students and give them multiple opportunities to practice and apply the strategies so that they are internalized and thus available to students outside of the specific lesson (NICHD, 2000). Many of these strategies support academic language development such as vocabulary strategies, reading comprehension strategies, and other language learning strategies. Think-alouds, during which teachers describe their thinking processes, offer an excellent way to demonstrate cognitive and metacognitive strategy use to students.

Some examples of what teachers can provide direct instruction on are listed below.

- **Vocabulary strategies**—Students need to learn strategies that will help them figure out new words they might encounter in text or speech. Context clues are one means, but are helpful only if the students know the other words in the vicinity of the unknown word. Examining the word for a possible cognate, word parts, or known similar words are other strategies. Reading on or listening further is another option because a new term may be defined later. Looking up a word in a glossary or dictionary is also helpful.

- **Reading comprehension strategies**—Students with literacy in their native language may need less instruction in the procedures for strategic ways to think about text they have read, but they do need practice in applying strategies they have to text in their new language. Students without such literacy need instruction starting at the basic level of comprehension. One thing that is important here is not only to teach students steps they can use in visualizing or summarizing, for example, but also to let them try these strategies with a variety of texts and genres.

- **Other language learning strategies**—Students can self-monitor when they read to make sure they get the gist of the text as they move along or reread what they have written to make sure it clearly conveys their ideas and is cohesive. They can monitor others' language use, such as by editing a peer's written work and checking for specific academic language elements. They can rehearse before they speak and draft before they write. They can analyze patterns in academic English and apply them to their own work. They can use non-verbal cues to understand language input.

For this feature to be well implemented teachers need to refer to strategies frequently. They may describe their thinking processes as they read aloud, solve a math problem, or hypothesize before a science experiment. They need to model the strategic thinking and then give students a chance to do the same with a similar problem or text. Teachers should also ask students to articulate the strategies they used to generate an answer.

 SIOP® Feature #14

Scaffolding Techniques

Through scaffolding, teachers enable students to complete tasks and move them toward independence. This gradual move happens in small steps. Sometimes the scaffolding is to help students understand procedures (e.g., use the illustrations to follow the steps for making a flip book) and sometimes it is to help students understand the new material being taught (e.g., take notes on this Venn diagram about the similarities and differences between the American and French Revolutions). Our interest here is the scaffolding teachers do to advance students' language proficiency. We refer to it as *verbal scaffolding*.

Some examples of verbal scaffolding include:

- Modeling correct speech.

- Paraphrasing what a student has said in order to subtly correct a pronunciation mistake, a verb tense, a malapropism, or the like.

- Prompting students to elaborate on an idea or generate a particular vocabulary word. (With young children this process might involve letting them express a concept in everyday language but teaching them how to say it more academically later [Gibbons, 2002]).

- Helping students describe relationships between ideas, using conjunctions like *although*, *however*, and *except*.

- Providing charts with signal words and sentence starters in the room and calling attention to them to support this language development.

Often these verbal scaffolds are unplanned. Teachers find a teachable moment in the class interaction and take advantage of it.

Other verbal scaffolds can be planned within the lesson:

- Showing students how to use language tools like a dictionary, a thesaurus, and a spell checker as part of any lesson that involves writing.

- Offering a series of guiding questions to help students understand a text or draft a piece of writing.

- Providing a partially completed outline for students to add to while they watch a video or listen to a speech to organize the new information.

As with construction scaffolds, success is achieved when the scaffolds are removed and the building stands on its own. These verbal scaffolds are designed to support students as they move to higher levels of language proficiency. After students master certain sentence starters, for example, the charts can be removed from the walls. When students realize teachers won't accept one- or two-word responses, they will begin to provide more elaborate answers.

 # SIOP® Feature #15

Variety of Questions for Higher-Order Thinking

Feature 15 emphasizes higher-order thinking and posing questions of various types in lessons. At first glance it may appear to have a less direct relationship to language development because the focus seems to be on *thinking*. However, students need to listen and participate in academic talk in order to discuss their critical reasoning. Open-ended, higher-order questions by their very nature require more language knowledge to understand the intent of the question and to produce a response.

As students begin to learn a new language, they often translate questions into their native language, think of an answer, and then translate that response into the new language before replying. This is not a very efficient method, but until students' language abilities get stronger, it is a necessary process. Given that the majority of teacher questions only require brief responses, such an effort is not always visible or time-consuming. This feature, however, reminds teachers that questions that require elaboration, justification, evaluation, application, and so on are more valuable for students, not only to gain deep understanding of the content being taught but also to develop more sophisticated language skills.

Students learning English are capable of higher-order thinking even though they may not always be able to express their thoughts completely. English learners need teacher support to understand the intent of some higher-order questions and to articulate their ideas in academic English. Think back to the discussion of academic language in Chapter 1. Academic language calls for decoding meaning—in this case, figuring out what the question or task is asking—and then encoding meaning—giving life to one's thoughts so they may be shared with others. Goals of academic language include being able to communicate complex reasoning and describe abstract concepts. Teachers can help students process and respond to higher-order questions and tasks in the following ways:

- Point out clues identifying that critical thinking is called for in the question or task, such as words related to cause and effect, comparison and contrast, problem and solution, alternatives, connections, and applications.

- Model how to respond to these questions, both orally and in writing.

- Provide language frames that correspond to the type of response expected, such as "One reason is . . ." to justify or persuade and "The text says . . . and I know . . . , so _____" to infer.

- Set aside time in lessons to explicitly work on comprehending and responding to higher-order questions; don't just throw some questions out to the class in the middle of a discussion.

ACTIVITY

Try this activity. Select a text passage from any content area and practice writing higher-order questions that are appropriate for your English learners. Be sure to use a variety of types including those that:

- Elicit language—*What is the author's purpose? Tell me why you think so.*
- Point out clues—*Notice the word, however. This is one of our signal words. It tells us there is something to contrast. What are the two things that are being contrasted in the sentence? How do they differ?*
- Clarify thinking—*How is that important? Why do you think _____ ? Can you give me a few more details?*
- Connects to an idea or another student's contribution—*Can you add something to what _____ said? How would you compare your idea to _____ ? What might be another point of view based on the text?*

Interaction

The Interaction component is closely focused on the development and use of academic language. Talk is an important way for us to process and retrieve information, discuss our ideas and extend our thoughts, describe what we observe and question what we don't. Through talk we can share our vision of the future as well as our evaluations of the past. When we engage in talk with others, we can deepen our knowledge, make sense of what we are reading or hearing, and improve the tasks we are completing (Vygotsky, 1978).

The Interaction component is very important for English learners who have to meet state standards, such as the Common Core, and English language proficiency standards, such as WIDA (World-class Instructional Design and Assessment). Standards related to Speaking and Listening can be explored through engaging academic talk that is scaffolded so that English learners can articulate their ideas and develop expressive language that allows them to sound like a historian, scientist, book critic, or mathematician.

Interaction

16. Frequent opportunities for interaction and discussion between teacher/student and among students, which encourage elaborated responses about lesson concepts.

17. Grouping configurations support language and content objectives of the lesson.

19. Ample opportunities for students to clarify key concepts in L1 as needed with aide, peer, or L1 text.

 SIOP® Feature #16

Frequent Opportunities for Interaction and Elaboration

This feature offers one of the best opportunities for teachers to help students develop academic listening and speaking skills in English. Part of the participation needed for full engagement in an academic conversation will come from socializing students to classroom interaction patterns. Teachers cannot assume that all students, especially, for example, newly arrived immigrants, will understand expectations for speaking up in American classrooms. If they have been in school in another country, they may have experienced teaching methods that rely on teachers telling students what to learn and students rotely memorizing information. Asking a teacher a question or posing a contrary opinion might have been dismissed as inappropriate behavior. Some students may never have been to school before. Moreover, even for those who have been in classrooms where academic talk between teacher and students happens regularly, getting a turn to talk and expressing an idea in a new language can still be a major barrier to participation. Therefore teachers should guide students toward the interaction desired.

This feature reminds teachers to include more techniques that require student–student interaction in their lessons, such as cooperative groups, pair work, activities that have students mingle and find partners to share ideas or information, role-plays, and simulations. Instead of leading whole class question and answer sessions, teachers are encouraged to try think-pair-share or turn-and-talk techniques so more students can practice their oral language skills. Small changes like these promote more student talk about the academic concepts.

While teachers sometimes focus on the first part of the feature—interaction between teacher and students and among students—the second half is even more important for advancing students' skills. The elaboration aspect of oral interaction is the means by which students can express their ideas fully, make connections between ideas or opinions or claims, embed an idea within another idea, make counterarguments, and much more.

The traditional classroom discussion—where the teacher dominates by asking questions, accepting one- or two-word responses, and then elaborating for the class—is not acceptable. It will not lead students to the rigorous level of discussion required by standards such as the Common Core, nor will it give those who need oral language practice (i.e., the students) time to practice when the teacher's words fill the air. Teachers should not elaborate on a student's brief response, but rather ask a follow-up question, like "What do you mean by that?" or "Can you tell me more?" And they need to ask more of the students. After solving a math problem, for example, the teacher should have the students explain the steps orally.

To build student academic talk, teachers can present language frames linked to the language functions relevant to the lesson task. For example, if students were to discuss causation in science, they could be taught to use frames like:

"The cause of _____ was . . . ."

"As a result of _____, . . . happened."

"_____ led to . . . ."

If they were to make a connection with texts they have read in language arts, they could use frames like these:

"The setting in the first book reminds me of . . . ."

"The first article said _____, but the second article reported . . . ."

"The characters in both books are similar in that they . . . ."

We hypothesize that as students become comfortable using these frames in oral interactions, they will start to use the frames in their writing and also recognize them in their readings.

SIOP® Feature #17

Grouping Configurations That Support the Language Objective

A common scene in a classroom is of desks grouped in sets of four or five. Students sit together but are not required to work together. They may share answers or ask a few questions, but typically they work on their own worksheets and interact very little. The physical structure of the classroom may look promising, but without planned collaborative activities it does not result in academic language development.

This feature connects the student groupings to the language objectives of the lesson. If the objective calls for discussion about a particular topic or use of new vocabulary terms, then the grouping and the task need to facilitate that. We have found that students use academic language more with strategic grouping and established routines.

- Teachers should consider reading ability (in the native language and in English) and English proficiency when pairing students. The higher-level partners may work more independently while the teacher spends more time supporting the less proficient pairs (Vaughn et al., 2009).

- Teachers must not only assign distinct roles to the students but also explain to them how to speak in the way their role requires as well as how to listen to their classmates and respond appropriately.

- Teachers can incorporate information gap activities in their lessons. In these cases, all students have only part of the necessary information and so must collaborate orally with partners to complete a task.

 SIOP® Feature #19

Native Language Use for Clarification

A student's native language is a resource that should be harnessed. It is another tool in a student's toolbox for understanding and processing new information. Research indicates when students have literacy in their native language, it helps them develop literacy in English more easily (Riches & Genesee, 2006). Teachers can encourage students to continue to develop their native language skills, even if the school does not offer bilingual courses, because the benefits will accrue. Certain skills, such as reading comprehension skills, will transfer from the native language to the new one.

For students whose native language has a Latin or Greek origin, their language may come in handy when trying to determine the meaning of unknown words since so many word parts in English have origins in those languages. Teachers will want to call attention to cognates and roots, for example, that some of their students might apply in these situations.

The use of bilingual glossaries and dictionaries, as well as electronic translators, can help students clarify information that is unclear to them and can help them build knowledge about the English language, too. They can learn multiple meanings and nuances of words. These tools offer another way for students to discover cognates and roots that their native language and English may have in common.

In Chapter 5 we continue the discussion on interaction and explore ways to promote more oral interaction among all of our students and help them meet standards for speaking and listening, like those required in the Common Core.

Practice & Application

The Common Core State Standards in English Language Arts and Mathematics, as well as the Next Generation Science Standards, place a premium on the application of knowledge. These standards want students not only to learn key topics, but also to be able to use that knowledge through guided and independent practice.

> **Practice & Application**
>
> **21.** Activities provided for students to apply content and language knowledge in the classroom.
>
> **22.** Activities integrate all language skills (i.e., reading, writing, listening, and speaking).

 ## SIOP® Feature #21

Activities to Apply Content and Language Knowledge

Feature 21 focuses on application of content and language knowledge. This means the students have had some practice and now are applying what they have learned to a new context. It is particularly important to give the students opportunities to explore how academic language works in new situations. We might, for instance, teach students how to read a text selection and determine the main idea and supporting details in a piece of fiction; we also would want to give them the experience of applying that reading skill to a science article, an advertisement, a poem, or another genre. As another example, consider a student learning math vocabulary and phrases that can be used to describe a bar graph. They may practice with one graph (Figure 2.2)

Figure 2.2 Class Votes for Healthy Snacks

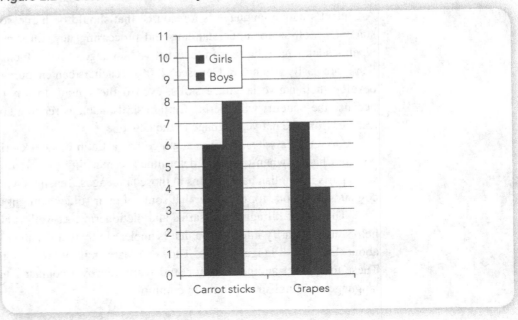

and learn to describe the graph with sentences such as "The bar representing girls' vote for grapes is three points higher than the bar showing the boys' vote" or "The graph shows that boys prefer carrots to grapes by 8 to 4." An application task may have them describe a similar graph to a partner or write a summary of the information shown in the graph.

Enabling students to conduct application activities is one way to move them toward independence. We are asking our English learners to produce and practice new language and vocabulary, but we are doing so in the supportive environment of a classroom before they must do so on their own.

 SIOP® Feature #22

Activities That Integrate all Language Skills

Language is the key to learning, whether it is in school, with a parent, or on the job. We primarily learn through reading, writing, listening, and/or speaking. We check our understanding mostly through language as well. For these reasons we want all SIOP teachers to develop lessons that integrate the four language skills. These four language skills are mutually supportive; working on one can shore up the others. It is a syncretic learning process (Genesee, Lindholm-Leary, Saunders, & Christian, 2006; Hinkel, 2006).

This feature does not imply that teachers need to have four language objectives each day, one per domain. No, one language objective is generally sufficient for explicit instruction in class. This feature intends for teachers to plan activities that encourage students to use their developing language skills of reading, writing, listening, and speaking to some extent during each lesson.

Take advantage of the opportunities these features have to engage students in meaningful tasks that integrate language and content. Student motivation will be enhanced if the activities have some authenticity and academic relevance, too. Many activities can integrate and apply the language skills in the service of deepening students' content knowledge. Several examples include:

- **TV Talk Show:** Guests on a talk show can represent experts who have to explain, persuade, or give opinions about a current event or real-life issue. Language frames that match the language function (e.g., persuasion) can support the interaction.

- **Book Club:** Students read different books or articles or websites and come together to summarize or discuss what they have learned as related to a research question or theme. A graphic organizer could be used while reading to record information.

- **Travel Agency:** Student groups prepare travel itineraries for clients that take them back in time to visit historical sites. They may prepare a travel brochure and maps. Or, they may simulate a tour with a guide describing the sites.

- **Press Room:** Students prepare a special edition of a newspaper or TV broadcast with articles/news segments and advertisements related to the lesson or unit content topic(s).

Lesson Delivery

Earlier we explained the importance of careful planning when designing lessons with English learners in mind. Those lessons need careful implementation as well; teachers must continually adjust their speech and scaffolds for the activities based on their assessment of student learning. In the Lesson Delivery component, we monitor the success of a lesson in helping students meet objectives.

> **Lesson Delivery**
>
> **24.** Language objectives clearly supported by lesson delivery.

 SIOP® Feature #24

Language Objectives Supported

Supporting the language objective means following through on the plans made for addressing the objective instructionally back in the Lesson Preparation phase. This feature holds teachers accountable. Did they help the students meet the language objective? Did the teachers teach to it? We can't promote students' language development if we don't provide explicit instruction in elements of academic language from time to time and if we don't give students multiple opportunities to practice and use the language in a variety of contexts.

If the lesson as it unfolded did not support language learning among the students, it is useful to examine why. Sometimes a lesson doesn't go as planned. Students may not grasp a concept as readily as expected and more time is needed to explore the new material. Sometimes a teacher assumes students can meet an objective (e.g., write a letter to the editor protesting teen curfews), but fails to provide explicit guidance in how to do so. One recommendation for teachers to keep students on track with their language development is to refer back to objective(s) during the lesson. The following suggestions may help:

- Reread the objective using shared reading during the lesson to re-focus the students.
- Ask students what they have done up to that point in the lesson that relates to the objective.
- *commonly seen* Have students rate how well they are meeting the objective, using informal checks. For example: Thumbs up ~ I got it. Thumbs down ~ I am completely lost. Thumbs sideways horizontally ~ I'm making progress.

Review & Assessment

This component has several features that relate to academic language development: the review of key vocabulary (Feature 27), the provision of feedback to students on their language output (Feature 29), and the assessment of student learning as related to the language objective (Feature 30). As we increase the rigor of our instruction, we must regularly monitor student learning. Formative assessments of both the content and language goal(s) of a lesson must be implemented.

> **Review & Assessment**
>
> **27.** Comprehensive review of key vocabulary.
>
> **29.** Regular feedback provided to students on their output (e.g., language, content, work).
>
> **30.** Assessment of student comprehension and learning of all lesson objectives (e.g., spot checking, group response) throughout the lesson.

SIOP® Feature #27

Review of Key Vocabulary

Because vocabulary knowledge is so important for conceptual understanding and success in school, we include this feature in the Review & Assessment component. First, we know students need repeated practice with new vocabulary words, and we believe that reminding the teacher to review these words at the end of a lesson offers an opportunity for engagement with the new terms. Second, we know that students often receive an overwhelming amount of input in their new language in each lesson and having the teacher point out the key vocabulary and concepts for students to remember helps keep them focused on the big picture.

Spending 3–5 minutes at the end of class can be a rewarding way to grow students' vocabulary repertoire. There are many techniques to do so, as these few examples indicate:

- Play a vocabulary game like *Pictionary*, bingo, charades, 20 questions, word splash, and word generation (more games can be found in the *Making Content Comprehensible for English Learners* and *99 Ideas* books).
- Have students write a sentence using the word on an exit slip.
- List new and old words on the board, and have students choose two to make a sentence.
- Give students a category and ask them to generate a list of related words, including new words and ones previously taught.

A word of caution is merited here. As we wrote in *Making Content Comprehensible* (Echevarria, Vogt & Short, 2013, p. 216):

> Please remember that effective review does not include the "dreaded word list" . . . nor the equally ineffective assignment of having students write vocabulary or spelling words ten (or more) times each. Research findings are very clear—isolated word lists and dictionary definitions alone do not promote vocabulary and language development.

SIOP® Feature #29

Regular Feedback on Student Output

Content teachers generally give students sufficient feedback on their understanding of curriculum topics or task assignments, but they are less apt to give feedback on students' use of academic language. While they might help with pronunciation or finding the right verb tense, they rarely correct the syntax of a sentence if it is comprehensible or push the students to elaborate their sentences into more fully formed thoughts that might warrant the use of conjunctions, relative clauses, logical connectors, and so on. Teachers often accept a one- or two-word answer from a student and provide the elaboration themselves.

At times teachers do not want to call attention to a student's linguistic error. Sometimes doing so will interrupt the flow of the lesson or take the discussion off on a tangent; sometimes doing so will, in the teacher's mind, embarrass the student in front of his or her classmates; and sometimes the teacher is unsure how to explain or correct the error. In the first case, teachers can make time later, perhaps in another lesson, to address the language error. If a number of students would benefit, a mini-lesson explicitly focusing on the grammar point or language usage issue may be called for. In the second case, the teacher can pull the student aside to arrange a time to talk about the error outside the class period or during time that students are working independently. Modeling is another way to provide feedback on accurate language use. Teachers can correctly restate the statement the student made, thus validating the student's utterance but also demonstrating the correct form or pronunciation. In the third case, the content teacher may want to let the ESL teacher know about the error and ask him or her to address it. That ESL teacher may also be able to tell the content teacher whether the error is a typical language acquisition issue and is something that is more likely to be learned when the student is more proficient in English.

One reason we are experiencing more long-term English learners in districts across the United States is because their academic language skills are "good enough" to get by in a content classroom but they don't reach an advanced or transitional level of English language proficiency. Giving students explicit feedback, and not accepting an answer that approximates what should be said, especially for students who are at an intermediate proficiency level or beyond, will help them in the long run.

We also want to point out that feedback can be offered regarding class and group participation. By giving feedback to students as they work together in groups, teachers can guide them to use the type of language associated with individually assigned roles. In order to help students take responsibility for their own academic language development, teachers can also instruct students in ways they can provide feedback to one another. Then activities like peer editing of written work and peer rating of oral presentations can be incorporated into lessons. These activities work best when peers not only indicate what needs to be improved but also express how it may be improved.

SIOP® Feature #30

Assessment of Student Comprehension

When we coach teachers, one important question we ask after an observation is "When did learning occur?" An effective SIOP teacher is able to answer this question, in part because she or he has regularly assessed the students' progress toward meeting the content and language objectives. Informal checks of comprehension and performance throughout the lesson inform teachers about which students may need some reteaching and which ones are able to move forward.

While this feature refers to both the content and language objectives, we are concerned with the assessment of academic language in this chapter . Some teachers may not feel comfortable assessing students' language development, but if they are taking the SIOP Model to heart, they need to give equal time to assessing both the students' content knowledge and their ability to use academic language to discuss and demonstrate their knowledge of the lesson topics as well as their facility with using academic language in appropriate ways. Sometimes we find that English learners do know the information on which they are being assessed, but because of language proficiency issues, including low vocabulary, reading, and writing skills, they are unable to demonstrate their knowledge fully. We encourage teachers to find accommodations to the language barriers that assessments raise. Multiple indicators—a number of different options for students to show their knowledge—are recommended.

Other ways to assess student learning of the language objective include:

- Have students rate and express their learning for the day, indicating with their fingers 1, 2 or 3:

  1. I can use the new academic language. For example . . .

2. I can want to know more about . . .

3. I need more help with . . .

> **ACTIVITY**
>
> Return to the lesson plan you looked at earlier in this chapter. How can you improve the opportunities for students to develop or practice their academic language development? Think of 2 or 3 ways to maximize their language learning.

2. I can want to know more about . . .

3. I need more help with . . .

- Have student groups do a Round Robin activity (talking consecutively for a specified time; or writing on, then passing around a single sheet of paper) about the aspect of academic English they learned in that lesson, or can do (e.g., generate sentences using the language target of the lesson).

- Before students leave the classroom, have them complete a Tickets Out card (also known as an Exit Slip) telling what they learned and/or asking any clarifying questions they need answered.

Summary

As you plan and deliver lessons that integrate content with language learning, features from the SIOP Model can keep academic language development on track. Working through lesson planning carefully can help ensure that English learners have multiple opportunities to learn and practice the language associated with the content topics and tasks. Remember the following points:

- Recognize that language learning opportunities occur frequently in every lesson. Learn to spot each opportunity and capitalize on it.

- Plan for instruction in elements and uses of academic language.

- Be explicit and model the type of academic language you want students to acquire.

- Remember that a well-crafted SIOP lesson with meaningful activities offers English learners and other students who need to strengthen their academic language and literacy:
  o targeted practice in academic language skills
  o instruction that matches the linguistic skills needed for processing the lesson's conceptual information or conducting the lesson's tasks.

Questions for Reflection

1. Write down the eight components of the SIOP Model. Under each, summarize the features that focus specifically on language development. Which component(s) do you typically implement in lessons? Which one is less familiar to you? How will you begin to incorporate those features into lessons?

2. Describe three types of learning strategies that support academic language development. Which strategy will you teach students to use at the beginning of the school year? Which might you teach later in the year?

3. Make an audio recording of your own teaching or use an available recorded lesson. How clear and understandable is the speech? Is there differentiation for various proficiency levels, such as simplified sentence structure for beginning speakers? Does the teacher modulate his or her speech to increase students' oral comprehension? What suggestions would you give to the teacher?

4. Make an action plan. What are two ways you will try to maximize the academic language development of your students over the next few months?

3 Strengthening Language Objectives

In this chapter you will

Content Objectives:

- Identify four categories of language objectives
- Determine how to differentiate instruction while keeping the same objectives for all students

Language Objectives:

- Write language objectives based on identified language targets
- Read language objectives and decide how each objective translates to instruction

The message we want to reinforce in this book is that academic language is a second language for all learners in school. Given that, all students benefit from attention to language development, even classes where both English learners and English speakers are present. In this chapter, we highlight the importance of including language objectives in all lessons so that students can develop and strengthen the language and literacy skills they need for academic success. In order for this to happen, teachers must plan carefully, teach explicitly to the language objectives, and offer multiple opportunities for academic language practice.

We are pleased when teachers begin to add language objectives to their lessons even if they are not worded with discrete language targets. Just having teachers think about language as one goal in a lesson is valuable. A teacher new to the process might write an objective such as "Students will discuss the plot of a story in groups" or "Students will write vocabulary sentences." If the teacher follows through and carves out time during the lesson for students to discuss the story's plot or use new vocabulary, that is a great leap forward in promoting academic language development.

This chapter will help teachers become more purposeful in planning their language objectives. It is designed to move teachers beyond writing general language objectives (such as those above) and toward creating more specific ones. Further, it will help them plan and execute lessons that let students meet those objectives. A strong language objective is the engine that drives language learning in a given class period. After reviewing some basic guidelines about objectives, we will discuss the following topics:

- how to recognize language objectives
- categories of language objectives
- language targets
- how to identify language objectives from text, talk, tasks, and tests
- how to write language objectives
- how to meet language objectives in lessons

Basic Guidelines for Identifying and Incorporating Objectives in SIOP Lessons

Figure 3.1 sets forth some basic guidelines about developing and using objectives in SIOP lessons. As we have mentioned in *Making Content Comprehensible for English Learners: The SIOP Model* (Echevarria, Vogt, & Short, 2013), the objectives are derived from state standards and student needs. They are not tangential to the instruction, but are an integral part of it. When students practice and meet objectives that are explicit learning targets, they advance their knowledge base. Objectives, it is critical to understand, are not activities; they are not the tasks the students are doing in the lesson. Objectives are the learning targets related to the content and language students need to accomplish the activities.

Content objectives are often easier for content teachers to write because they typically come directly from the curricular frameworks of the subject areas. Language objectives, the main focus of this chapter, are more daunting for content teachers because there are so

Figure 3.1   Basic Guidelines to Identify Objectives and Incorporate Them in Lessons

1. All the content and language objectives should evolve from the lesson topic and be part of the instructional plan. However, an objective is not a by-product of an activity but the foundation of one.
2. Each objective is what we want the students to learn—a language target.
3. We determine content objectives from state standards for subject areas.
4. We can determine language objectives from state standards for English language proficiency and by considering the (a) language of the texts students will read or write (including vocabulary, grammar, functional language), (b) language of the talk teachers use to convey new information, (c) language students must produce to practice or demonstrate their knowledge, and (d) language of the tests students take.
5. We write objectives using active verbs and include the language target. We avoid the verbs *learn, understand,* and *comprehend*; these verbs are difficult to observe directly.
6. We post and discuss objectives with students. *Remember:* Writing an agenda or list of activities on the board is not the same as writing the content and language objectives!
7. At some point in the lesson, we provide explicit instruction on these objectives, both for content and language.
8. We plan and deliver lessons with opportunities for students to practice with the objectives and be assessed on their progress toward meeting them.

many possibilities for every lesson. For ESL or ELD (English language development) teachers, the opposite might prove true. Their language objectives are more easily determined from their curricula but they need to identify content to complement the lesson. Some teachers who have a separate ESL class might draw from one content area or focus on one subject per quarter. Others might intermingle content areas and focus on academic tasks needed in those subjects (e.g., reading a textbook, writing a research paper, recording observations, explaining steps in an equation). Overall, it is critical to remember the following:

- Content objectives are the *what*, what students need to learn about the content topic
- Language objectives are the *what* too, what students need to learn about English in order to
  - ○ learn, share, or apply new information
  - ○ demonstrate knowledge
  - ○ perform academic tasks

It is important to use active verbs in our objectives. These verbs convey to students that they are participants in the learning process. We want our objectives to be measurable and observable. Therefore, we do not use verbs like *learn, understand,* or *comprehend* in our objective statements. These verbs represent what may be going on in the heads of students, but they are not directly observable to the teacher.

Within the lesson, either at the start or early on, we post our objectives and discuss them with students. This practice works best when teachers allot some time for that discussion. They don't just read the objectives aloud and move on; rather, they spend a few minutes explaining how the objectives fit into the lesson and/or the unit being studied and perhaps what activities will support the objectives. Students can paraphrase the objectives to a partner or share an idea of how the objective might be applied. What is *not* equivalent to posting objectives is writing the agenda for the period on the board—a routine teachers have traditionally followed. Some teachers may want to post both objectives and agenda, but the objectives cannot be overlooked.

As the lesson goes on, we expect teachers to instruct on the objectives. In other words, at some point in the lesson the teacher explicitly teaches to the content and language objectives. This may involve introducing a new skill, setting up a practice opportunity, or reviewing the targets in the objectives with the students. The activities within the lesson that allow students to practice with the objectives should not be relegated to homework assignments. They should occur within the class period so the teacher can provide feedback to students on how well they are meeting them. Informally teachers should assess if students have mastered the objectives and decide if reteaching is needed or if they can move forward with the unit.

Recognizing Language Objectives

Look at the following exercise. Mark the statements in this way: Place an **LO** if the statement is a language objective and an **A** if it is an activity.

 1. Students will be able to orally explain the difference between living and non-living things.

 2. At the end of this lesson, students will have learned to set up a Bunsen burner, fill a graduated cylinder, and use a triple balance.

_LO_   3. Students will be able to define the meaning of these words: debate, veto, bill.

_A_   4. Children will read at least 3 of 6 fables with a partner.

_A_   5. Students will take notes.

A key point to remember in effective planning and teaching is that a language objective is not an activity. It needs to be something a teacher addresses instructionally and that students learn, or make progress in learning. Hence, it is a learning goal related to language. Of the statements above, we would say that #1 and #3 are language objectives. They tell what language function students will employ (oral explanation, definition) and what the target of the language use is (differences between living and non-living things, specific vocabulary words). #3 could be modified slightly to include defining the terms orally, or in writing, or both modes, but such specificity is not always necessary, especially if not stating the mode allows for some needed differentiation among the students.

Statement #2 is an activity for a science lesson. Surely the science teacher wants students to be able to do these three things, but they could be taught and mastered without language use at all, just by mimicking a demonstration. To turn this statement into a language objective, a teacher might write "Students will read and follow directions in order to set up a Bunsen burner, fill a graduated cylinder, and use a triple balance." It would be a reasonable one if the students do not know how to read and follow directions or if they need further support in doing so, which would then be the focus of the instruction.

Statements #4 and #5 have potential to be language objectives, and indeed might be something a teacher new to the concept might write. Both involve a language skill (reading, writing), which is positive. But what are the learning goals within these statements? For #4, does the teacher want students to simply read with a partner? How will the teacher know if the pairs accomplish the task? Because at least three fables are read? Does comprehension of what is read matter? Or does the teacher want students to practice reading aloud, perhaps to build fluency or work on word recognition? The issue with #5 is similar. Learning to take notes is an important goal for students in school, yes, but what are they taking notes from? Are they reading and taking notes about key ideas? Are they listening to a speech and jotting down details about a particular topic? Are they taking notes to prepare for an oral presentation they will do? The wording of both statements is too vague.

Depending on the students' needs and the teacher's plan for language learning in the unit, possible revised objectives could be the following:

4a. Students will read at least 3 fables orally to a partner with correct intonation and pronunciation, or

4b. Students will read at least 3 fables to a partner and evaluate how relevant the messages are to daily life.

5a. Students will listen to and watch a video on natural disasters and record two facts about each, or

5b. Students will write steps for how to do something on note cards to practice giving a How To speech.

Categories of Language Objectives

In our work with the SIOP Model, we enumerate four categories of language objectives for teachers to consider: Academic Vocabulary, Language Skills and Functions, Language Structures or Grammar, and Language Learning Strategies. We recommend they develop objectives from these categories over the course of a unit. The first category, Academic Vocabulary, is the easiest for teachers to grasp. All teachers are used to teaching vocabulary, and textbooks typically boldface the content and technical words. We remind teachers that while vocabulary is very important to teach, it is not all the language a student needs to become proficient in academic English.

These four categories are briefly explained below.

Academic Vocabulary.   Key words needed to discuss, read, or write about the lesson topic.

- *Content vocabulary:* These key words and technical terms are subject specific and often comprise the highlighted words in textbooks. Students need them to understand lesson concepts, but they may be low-frequency words, particularly in high school courses.

- *General academic vocabulary:* These words include cross-curricular academic terms (e.g., *event, result, observe*), transition words and logical connectors (e.g., *however, because, next*), and language function words (e.g., *compare, persuade*). This category includes medium- and high-frequency words that are used in academic and social conversations.

- *Word parts:* This category refers to roots, prefixes, and suffixes. Attention to the structure of words can help expand a student's vocabulary knowledge considerably. For example, if a student knows that *vis* is the root meaning "to see," they can begin to guess the meaning of words like *vision, visual, invisible,* and *visualize.*

In a lesson, the teacher spends time making sure students become familiar with the definitions and can use the words, with support as needed. The teacher regularly reviews key unit words.

Language Skills and Functions.   The reading, writing, listening, and speaking skills students need to understand and convey meaning in a lesson and the students' purpose for using language.

- English learners need direct and progressive instruction in the four language skills and opportunities to practice. The skills (and subskills) taught need to link to the topic of the lesson. In a language arts class, for example, will students need to read and find evidence in the text to support a claim? In social studies, will they need to watch a video recording and identify details from a historical conflict?

- Students have to use language for specific purposes in a lesson—to describe, compare, or predict, for example. English learners need instruction particularly in models (e.g., academic language frames) to articulate their descriptions or comparisons or predictions.

If a lesson focuses on a language skill, the teacher considers subskills to teach. For example, in writing, students may need to begin with forming letters of the alphabet, and then move to forming words, phrases, sentences, and finally paragraphs. Students need to learn to edit their writing by focusing on word choice or audience and so forth. For a lesson on language functions, the teacher spends time teaching or reviewing the purpose and procedures for the targeted language use. The teacher might provide questions and starters or sentence frames (e.g., "What will happen when . . . ?" "Both of them are . . . " "I predict that . . .") to guide the students.

Language Structures or Grammar.   The patterns, structures, rules, and descriptions of expressions in a language. It includes parts of speech, sentence formation, usage, and punctuation.

- Teachers pay attention to the language structures in the written or spoken discourse of the subject (e.g., *if–then* clauses, superlative adjectives, passive voice) and teach the structures that are widely used to their students.

- Both content and language teachers will find that having a list of English language structures and grammar points (like a scope and sequence found in an ESL textbook) is a valuable reference tool. One difficulty with long-term English learners is that they plateau in their grammatical language development, never reaching advanced or native-like proficiency because they can "get by." Making sure they do not receive a "Swiss cheese" approach to language development—that is, making sure all the patterns and structures are taught over time—can help mitigate the potential for long-term status.

The teacher introduces or reviews the types of sentences or unfamiliar parts of speech in a text. Beginning level students need to understand that a statement like "Put the paper under the book" is a sentence that calls for an action specified by a particular preposition.

Language Learning Strategies.   Mental processes and ways of thinking that give students resources to learn on their own (Cohen, 1998).

> **Use Pop-up Objectives!**
>
> Have students write the day's objectives on a sticky note that has been folded so the sticky side will face down and adhere to the desktop. At the end of the day, ask students to add an assessment of their learning on the back and use it as a ticket out.

- Analytic strategies (e.g., use cognates, roots, or affixes to guess word meaning)
- Corrective strategies (e.g., reread confusing text)
- Self-monitoring strategies (e.g., make and confirm predictions)
- Prereading strategies (e.g., relate to personal experience, preview pictures)
- Language practice strategies (e.g., repeat or rehearse phrases, imitate a native speaker)

The teacher names and models these strategies and provides time in class for students to practice. From time to time, the teacher may also suggest a strategy for students to use for a particular task.

Language Targets

To help teachers generate language objectives based on these four categories, we have developed a Language Targets Chart. As teachers think through possible goals they have for students to learn academic English in several lessons or a unit, they can record their ideas in this organizer. Figure 3.2 is a sample of the kinds of language targets that could be developed more fully into language objectives.

Figure 3.2 **Sample Language Targets**

Academic Vocabulary	Language Skills & Functions
synonyms	making comparisons
sequence terms	asking questions
technical words	reading for specific information
Language Structures & Grammar	**Language Learning Strategies**
comparative adjectives/clauses	clarifying questions
if–then clauses	representing data
past-tense verbs	rehearsing

...pleted Language Targets Chart would be a resource for the teachers to use when writing their lessons and selecting the specific objectives for each one. Sometimes teachers find they do not include all the targets from the chart as the unit unfolds; sometimes they add other ones based on the needs they determine.

Identifying Language Objectives from Text, Talk, Tasks, and Tests

As teachers brainstorm which language targets to include in the chart, we suggest they consider the language students will be exposed to or asked to produce. These demands may be found in text students need to read, teacher talk that they will hear, tasks they will be required to perform, and tests they will take.

Language Targets in Text

By examining what students will be asked to read, teachers can determine if aspects of the academic language in the text might be problematic for the students based on their English proficiency levels and the content that has been taught up to that point in time. Consider the following paragraph from a middle school history book. What might cause comprehension problems for students reading this?

> Spanish conquistadors had brought horses and cattle to the Americas in the 1500s. Spaniards who lived in what is now the American Southwest employed local Native Americans, some of whom they called Pueblos, to tend their horses. Horses, and knowledge about riding them, spread from group to group. Once, Native Americans had hunted buffalo on foot, but with horses hunters could kill as many buffalo in a day as they had once killed in a week.
>
> (*U.S. History*, Globe Fearon, 1999, p. 127)

Teachers typically identify unknown vocabulary first, such as *conquistador, cattle, Pueblos, tend, spread,* and *buffalo.* Some of these words may be new terms and concepts to students: *conquistador, Pueblos, buffalo.* Some words may be new words for known concepts:

cattle for cows and bulls. Some may be multiple-meaning words and the meaning in the passage is new to students: *tend, spread*. And some are expressions that may confuse the students: *on foot*. Knowing their students, teachers can decide if some of these words need to be taught explicitly or can just be explained quickly as the reading takes place.

> Spanish **conquistadors** had brought horses and **cattle** to the Americas in the 1500s. Spaniards who lived in what is now the American Southwest employed local Native Americans, some of whom they called **Pueblos**, to **tend** their horses. Horses, and knowledge about riding them, **spread** from group to group. Once, Native Americans had hunted **buffalo on foot**, but with horses hunters could kill as many buffalo in a day as they had once killed in a week.
>
> *(U.S. History*, Globe Fearon, 1999, p. 127)

When asked to look at other aspects of the academic language in this text, teachers might start to see some syntax that could trip students up. Teachers notice the different verb tenses: simple past (*lived, employed, called*), the past perfect (*had brought, had hunted, had killed*), the infinitive (*to tend*), and the modal (*could*). Depending on the students' proficiency levels, teaching the past perfect or the modal might be needed.

> Spanish conquistadors *had brought* horses and cattle to the Americas in the 1500s. Spaniards who *lived* in what is now the American Southwest *employed* local Native Americans, some of whom they *called* Pueblos, *to tend* their horses. Horses, and knowledge about riding them, *spread* from group to group. Once, Native Americans *had hunted* buffalo on foot, but with horses hunters *could kill* as many buffalo in a day as they *had* once *killed* in a week.
>
> *(U.S. History*, Globe Fearon, 1999, p. 127)

We also see not only different ways to signal time in this paragraph, but also different time periods jumbled together. We have *in the 1500s*, which provides a specific century but implies the event (bringing horses) could have occurred multiple times in that time frame. The adverb *now* refers to the current time (or the time this text was written). And we have the vague adverb *once* used twice, meaning "in the past" (not the more commonly used meaning, "one time only"). *Once* can also be a conjunction, meaning "as soon as." Another conjunction, *but*, is in this paragraph too, and students will need to know it indicates a contrast between two ideas.

> Spanish conquistadors had brought horses and cattle to the Americas **in the 1500s.** Spaniards who lived in what is **now** the American Southwest employed local Native Americans, some of whom they called Pueblos, to tend their horses. Horses, and knowledge about riding them, spread from group to group. **Once**, Native Americans had hunted buffalo on foot, **but** with horses hunters could kill as many buffalo in a day as they had **once** killed in a week.
>
> *(U.S. History*, Globe Fearon, 1999, p. 127)

Embedded clauses, so emblematic of academic language, are frequent in this four-sentence paragraph. Learning how to break apart such dense text to improve comprehension is a skill that teachers can help students achieve. It is also a skill that will serve the students well throughout their academic lives. In the second sentence we have an embedded adjectival clause introduced by a relative pronoun (*who*) with a complex prepositional phrase (*who lived in what is now the American Southwes*t) and another relative clause introduced by a modifier (*some of*) (*some of whom they called Pueblos*). We have compound subjects as well (*Horses, and knowledge about riding them . . .*), which can challenge students to determine the subject of the sentence. Even certain prepositional phrases (e.g., *with horses*) can interfere with reading comprehension.

> Spanish conquistadors had brought horses and cattle to the Americas in the 1500s. Spaniards <u>who lived in what is now the American Southwest</u> employed local Native Americans, <u>some of whom they called Pueblos,</u> to tend their horses. <u>Horses, and knowledge about riding them,</u> spread from group to group. Once, Native Americans had hunted buffalo on foot, but <u>with horses</u> hunters could kill as many buffalo in a day as they had once killed in a week.
>
> *(U.S. History,* Globe Fearon, 1999, p. 127)

Below, we combine the potential grammatical and vocabulary pitfalls discussed so far in this single paragraph to illustrate the challenges students confront daily in their textbooks. Every sentence has at least two possible barriers to comprehension, particularly for beginning and intermediate level English learners. Certainly we are not asking the history teachers to teach the nuances of the grammar, but if they choose one of these topics as an area for a language objective, they may be able to offer some guidance in how to read the passage for understanding, by modeling using think-alouds, for instance. History teachers could also ask their ESL or language arts colleagues to address some of these issues in their classes.

> Spanish **conquistadors** *had brought* horses and **cattle** to the Americas *in the 1500s*. Spaniards <u>who lived in what</u> *is* **now** <u>the American Southwest</u> *employed* local Native Americans, <u>some of whom they called</u> **Pueblos, to tend** their horses. <u>Horses, and knowledge about riding them,</u> **spread** from group to group. ***Once***, Native Americans *had hunted* **buffalo on foot**, but <u>with horses</u> hunters *could kill* as many **buffalo** in a day as they *had* **once** *killed* in a week.
>
> *(U.S. History,* Globe Fearon, 1999, p. 127)

This analysis of the text can be converted into a Language Targets Chart, as seen in Figure 3.3. Although all of these possible targets are unlikely to be language objectives for

Figure 3.3   Language Targets for Social Studies Explorers Lesson

Academic Vocabulary	Language Skills & Functions
multiple-meaning words time-signal words	read to determine effects of Spanish colonization retell the sequence of events
Language Structures & Grammar	**Language Learning Strategies**
relative clauses past-perfect verbs	using a dictionary

the one lesson where students read this paragraph, one may be selected because it suits the students' language development needs. Further, some may be applicable to other passages in the chapter students are working on.

ACTIVITY

Identify the different types of academic language in this science textbook paragraph.

Energy is defined as the capacity to cause change—for instance, by doing work. Potential energy is the energy that matter possesses because of its location or structure. For example, water in a reservoir on a hill has potential energy because of its altitude. When the gates of the reservoir's dam are opened and the water runs downhill, the energy can be used to do work, such as turning generators. Because energy has been expended, the water has less energy at the bottom of the hill than it did in the reservoir. To restore the potential energy of a reservoir, work must be done to elevate the water against gravity. (*Biology*, Pearson, 2008, p. 35)

Language Targets in Talk

We know that teachers talk 70%–80% of the time in most classes. As a result, students need to develop strong listening comprehension skills. Language objectives related to talk may involve receptive skills, such as listening for specific information, or interactive skills such as listening and note-taking or listening and speaking in response to teacher talk. As you plan your lesson, think about what you will be saying to the students and how much of the new information will be conveyed orally. It is important for teachers to modulate their speech to match the proficiency levels of their students. They may also plan mini-lectures or explanations that can support the students' language development, not just add to their content knowledge.

Consider the following excerpt from a Grade 7 health class when the teacher orally introduces the day's topic:

> **Health Teacher:** Good morning class. Today we are going to learn about the effects of narcotics on the body. Narcotics are a class of drugs. In the U.S., they require a prescription for use. They are used to relieve pain. They are addictive. Often after someone has had major surgery, he or she is given a narcotic like Percocet to use during recovery. So, narcotics like Percocet or morphine can be used legally under a doctor's care. Some narcotics, like cocaine, are often used illegally.

Students will listen to this brief introduction and hear health-related words and defining characteristics of narcotics as well as some examples. Possible language targets that could be further developed in this lesson are shown in Figure 3.4.

Figure 3.4   Language Targets from Teacher Talk

Academic Vocabulary	Language Skills & Functions
narcotics, drugs, legally, illegally, addictive	listening for specific details
Language Structures & Grammar	**Language Learning Strategies**
adverbs ending in -*ly*	identify cognates

ACTIVITY

Imagine you are a math teacher. Write down an equation or word problem connected to the level of mathematics that you teach or are familiar with, such as

$$9.5 + 5.25 = 14.75 \qquad 9\tfrac{1}{2} + 5\tfrac{1}{4} =$$

$$or$$

$$4s + 16 = 36$$

Now record a think-aloud, explaining each step (as if to the class) as you solve the problem. Replay the recording and ask yourself if that is the academic oral language you want from your students. If it is, compare it with what you usually hear. What is different? What aspects of the academic math language are the students missing? This can become a source for a language objective.

Language Targets in Tasks

We can also select language objectives based on the language students need to have to accomplish tasks in a lesson or unit. Look at the activities that the teacher of this elementary language arts lesson has planned. Her fifth grade class has native English speakers and English learners, most of whom are at intermediate and advanced levels. What language demands will be present for the students?

Elementary Language Arts Lesson

In a prior lesson, students watched a video clip about different types of guide dogs and discussed how animals help humans. In this lesson, students read a newspaper article about a school board in Virginia considering whether a trained dog that can detect low blood sugar may be allowed to accompany a diabetic second grader to class. Student in pairs or small groups write a letter to the newspaper calling on schools to allow such dogs to accompany diabetic children.

In order to accomplish the task of writing a letter to the editor, the students will need to learn some academic vocabulary, such as *diabetes/diabetic* and *school board*, and some phrases related to persuasive speech, such as *It would be best . . .* , and *In our opinion, ...* The teacher might want to teach or review modals, such as *should, ought to,* and *must*, along with *if–then* statements. A possible language targets chart for this lesson is found in Figure 3.5.

Figure 3.5   Language Targets for Elementary Language Arts Lesson

Academic Vocabulary	Language Skills & Functions
health terms: diabetes, diabetic, low blood sugar	persuading
	reading for specific information
persuasive phrases: We recommend, In our opinion, It would be better	writing a letter to the editor
Language Structures & Grammar	**Language Learning Strategies**
modals (*should, ought to, must*)	visualize while reading
if–then clauses	editing
letter format	

The next example is a middle school math lesson that is part of an interdisciplinary STEM unit.

> ### Middle School Math Lesson
>
> The goal of this unit is to build a scale model of the planets and sun. Students have been studying the solar system in their science class. In math class, the main task is for student groups to calculate (1) scale models for the planets given a particular diameter of Earth and (2) the spacing of the planets so they are appropriate distances from the sun. The groups report on their calculations to the class. The students will work with their technology teacher to create graphic representations on the computer after their calculations are completed. Resources available to the students include the Internet and science and math textbooks.

To complete the task, students will need to know about ratios and proportions and scale models. They may need to generate hypotheses about the size of the planets in relation to the size of Earth and evaluate them when they calculate the size of different planets and their distances from the sun. Possible language targets for this lesson are found in the chart in Figure 3.6.

Figure 3.6   Language Targets for Middle School Math Lesson

Academic Vocabulary	Language Skills & Functions
math terms: ratio, proportion, scale, in relation to *academic phrases:* "Xx is four times bigger than yy," "Given that Earth is mmm, Mars must be . . ."	justifying explaining scanning for information in text
Language Structures & Grammar	**Language Learning Strategies**
comparative/superlative adjectives	drawing pictures and labeling

Language Targets in Tests

Many tests that our students take in school are multiple-choice. To understand the language of the testing items, students need to know key vocabulary, synonyms and antonyms, common language functions in the prompt or stem of the question, and often restrictors that narrow possible answers such as "All of the following are __ except . . ." and "Which of the following is *not* _____?"

The following two questions are public sample items reflecting the upcoming Grade 8 English language arts assessment prepared by the PARCC consortium to measure the Common Core standards for English language arts and literacy. In order to answer them, students were expected to read an excerpt from *Call of the Wild* by Jack London (provided as part of the assessment).

One thing to note is the use of *best* as a restrictor in both questions. Students will have to realize that this means there may be more than one answer, but of the possibilities, one is the best. As teachers, we need to help students figure out what would make one answer better

Part A Question: Which statement best reflects a theme of the excerpt from *Call of the Wild?*

    a. Survival is unlikely when one is new to an environment.

    b. Survival requires adapting to one's surroundings.

    c. One cannot rely on others when learning to survive.

    d. Advanced preparation is necessary for survival.

Part B Question: Which two details from the excerpt best support the answer in Part A?

    a. "Here and there savage dogs rushed upon him, but he bristled his neck-hair and snarled (for he was learning fast), and they let him go his way unmolested." (paragraph 1)

    b. "Again he wandered about through the great camp, looking for them, and again he returned." (paragraph 2)

    c. "He sprang back, bristling and snarling, fearful of the unseen and unknown." (paragraph 2)

    d. "Buck confidently selected a spot, and with much fuss and wasted effort proceeded to dig a hole for himself." (paragraph 3)

    e. "It was a token that he was harking back through his own life to the lives of his forebears . . ." (paragraph 4)

    f. ". . . he saw the white camp spread out before him and knew where he was . . ." (paragraph 4)

Source: Partnership for Assessment of Readiness for College and Careers (PARCC) and PearsonAccess C Copyright 1998–2015 Pearson Education, Inc. All rights reserved. http://parcc.pearson.com

than another. Does it give more details? Is it more generalizable? The answer will depend on the question and the context.

    We also see content-specific language, such as *theme* and *details*, and general academic terms, such as *reflects* and *support*, in the question stems. These types of terms are also present in the multiple-choice options. Part A's answer options include some negations (*unlikely*, *cannot*), synonyms (*environment*, *surroundings*), and subordinate clauses (*when* clauses), which students have to understand. The excerpted sentences in Part B's options are quite complex and display characteristics of academic text that we described in Chapter 1. Students who answer Part A correctly may struggle with Part B because of the difficult academic language.

    Possible language targets for a lesson related to these sample test questions appear in Figure 3.7.

Figure 3.7   Language Targets from Tests

Academic Vocabulary	Language Skills & Functions
synonyms question words restrictive terms (e.g., *best, except*)	read to determine what is being asked
Language Structures & Grammar	**Language Learning Strategies**
subordinate clauses	re-read and monitor read questions before passage

ACTIVITY

To help you generate language objectives, try the following brainstorming procedure. Reflect on an upcoming unit and list all the possible language objectives that could be taught, based on the texts and tasks you anticipate including in the unit lessons. Consider what you will say to explain new information to the students and any other audio input they may have. If you have a unit test already prepared, think about the embedded language there as well. Now record the possible language targets in the chart below. Remember to try to include targets across the four categories.

Language Targets Activity Chart

Academic Vocabulary	Language Skills & Functions
Language Structures & Grammar	Language Learning Strategies

Writing Language Objectives

After the teachers have generated targets for the chart, we suggest they use language frames to write the actual objective. Each of the following examples calls for an active verb and for a language target, which could be pulled from the chart.

> A. Students will **(function: active verb phrase)** using/with **(language target)**.
>
> B. Students will [use] **(language target)** to **(function: active verb phrase)**.
>
> C. Students will **(language target as active verb)** [with _____].

Here are some examples of these objectives from the charts above:

> A. Students will write a letter to the editor using prepositional phrases of time.
>
> B. Students will use synonyms to improve their writing.
>
> C. Students will rehearse a speech with a partner.

We do want to note that not all language objectives need to be written with these language frames. They are offered here as a guide for teachers so that the objectives are not simply language activities but have a language learning purpose as well. Like all language frames, they are scaffolds. As teachers become more comfortable writing objectives and more familiar with how academic language is used in their subjects and what their students need to learn, the teachers may no longer need to use these frames.

ACTIVITY

Look at the language targets you placed in your chart in the previous activity. Try to write two language objectives below based on those targets.

Meeting Language Objectives

One concern that we continue to have when we observe lessons is that teachers write language objectives and may even review them with the class, but they do not follow through. As we have stated repeatedly, there must be explicit instruction so students learn about the language target and practice it. Look at the chart in Figure 3.8.

In Chapter 2, we discussed the SIOP Model features that are directly related to academic language development. This relationship becomes important once teachers have written language objectives for their lesson plan: they must ensure that the lesson follows through with explicit instruction and practice opportunities for the students.

Figure 3.8 Explicit Instruction for Language Objectives

Language Objective	What It Means Instructionally
Academic Vocabulary: Students will define new vocabulary terms.	Teacher instructs students how to define a term: state attributes, give an example, draw a picture, or use in a sentence.
Language Skills and Functions: Students will ask questions about rock characteristics to determine a mystery rock.	Teacher instructs or reminds students how to pose questions and how to listen carefully by paying attention to key words. The teacher models the question-answer task.
Language Structures: Students will explain their experimental results using *if–then* statements.	Teacher shows students how to form an *if–then* statement. She models real causation scenarios (e.g., holds a ball and says, "If I drop this, the ball will hit the ground and bounce," and then does so). She creates two lists and has students join phrases/clauses together to create *if–then* statements.
Language Learning Strategies: Students will use the thesaurus to improve a peer's lab report.	Teacher explains how to use a thesaurus and models how to find synonyms to enliven a text. Using an example students would know, teacher explains all synonyms are not equal; they may have subtle differences to consider when selecting one to replace another word.

ACTIVITY

Read the examples below and explain the instructional implications.

Subject	Language Objective	What Does It Mean Instructionally?
Math	Students will orally list the steps for converting a fraction to a percent using sequence terms.	*Teacher models how to convert.*
Science	Students will make comparisons between the rock cycle and the water cycle with phrases like "Both are . . ." and "One has . . . but the other has . . . ."	*Teacher demonstrate both are ...*
Language Arts	Students will write a paragraph about a character's traits and actions.	*evidence, connectors, paragraph formats*
History	Students will read a textbook selection on the War of 1812 to find key events and supporting details.	*identify key events that are significant.*

Think about the following objective related to academic vocabulary in a language arts class, for example. Suppose the objective is "Students will summarize a passage using key vocabulary." Within the lesson the teacher defines key terms or reviews them with students (vocabulary: Feature #9) and plans a task where they will use the words in an authentic way, as through the summary (meaningful activities: Feature #6). The teacher may need to review steps for summarizing (higher-order thinking: Feature #15) and perhaps provides a model summary of another passage students are already familiar with or some summary paragraph frames for less proficient students (scaffolding: Feature #14). Perhaps students will work with partners or in small groups (student–student interaction: Feature #16) to accomplish this task, which gives them an opportunity to apply their language knowledge (application activities: Feature #21). At the end of the lesson, the students share their summaries, meeting the language objective (Feature #24) and reviewing the key vocabulary (Feature #27).

While it is critically important for teachers to follow through with objectives, both content and language, when delivering a lesson, it is also important to advance English learners' academic language proficiency. That is why we encourage teachers to choose objectives that move the students forward. Collaboration between language and content teachers is one way to make this happen. The ESL or ELD teacher should have a scope and sequence of language goals for the students that can be shared with the content teachers. If students have mastered basic reading comprehension, for instance, the teachers may move on to inferencing. If students can form basic subject-verb-object sentences, the teachers may show students how to add prepositional phrases of time or location to enhance the text.

Differentiate Instruction, Not Language Objectives

Over the years, teachers have asked us if the language objectives should be differentiated. We have always said no. Instead, differentiation should occur at the process stage—when teachers teach to the objective—or the product stage—when students demonstrate proficiency with the objective. The process stage involves the teacher's speech, her or his use of comprehensible input techniques, scaffolding, and more in order to provide explicit instruction that meets the students' level of understanding. Teachers can also prorate the task assigned, thus accommodating proficiency levels. Beginning-level students may be required to write one paragraph after conducting Internet research on a desert animal, while more advanced students write three paragraphs and native English speakers write a five-paragraph essay.

Consider the following scenario from an Algebra class. In this lesson, students are asked to solve some algebraic equations, the content objective. The teacher wants the students not only to show the steps they take to solve the equation but also to explain each step mathematically (the language objective). The following is the example the teacher plans to model: *The sum of twice a number plus 13 is 75. Find the number.* Students will then be asked to work in pairs to solve similar problems.

As the teacher thinks through this problem, she realizes there is quite a bit of academic language involved in doing the task, especially for her beginning-level English learners. Several vocabulary words should be reviewed to make sure their mathematical meanings are clear: *sum, twice, plus, is,* and *find.* The written solution is straightforward, but the oral explanation for each step might vary by proficiency level. She may, therefore, determine that less proficient students meet the objective if they explain their steps in this fashion:

> The sum of twice a number plus 13 is 75. Find the number.
>
> Oral explanation: *So I have a number x. I need two times x and I add 13. Then I will get 75.*
>
> Written solution and oral explanation of each step:
>
> $2x + 13 = 75$ *I write out the equation.*
>
> $2x + 13 - 13 = 75 - 13$ *I need to get x alone so I subtract 13 from both sides.*
>
> $2x = 62$ *I do the math.*
>
> $\frac{2x}{2} = \frac{62}{2}$ *I still need x alone so I divide both sides by 2.*
>
> $x = 31$ *I find that x equals 31.*

More advanced level students, however, would be encouraged to use explanations that are more like a mathematician's reasoning:

> The sum of twice a number plus 13 is 75. Find the number.
>
> Oral explanation: *Let the number be x. If I double x and add 13, it will equal 75.*
>
> Written solution and oral explanation of each step:
>
> $2x + 13 = 75$ *I convert the words to an equation.*
>
> $2x + 13 - 13 = 75 - 13$ *I isolate x by subtracting 13, the same amount, from both sides.*
>
> $2x = 62$ *I simplify.*
>
> $\frac{2x}{2} = \frac{62}{2}$ *I isolate x by dividing both sides by 2.*
>
> $x = 31$ *The result is that x equals 31.*

In this manner, the teacher can demonstrate multiple ways to explain the problem that adjust for the students' developing English skills (meeting the language objective) yet also verify that the students are able to solve the math problem (meeting the content objective).

Summary

As we prepare our students for colleges and careers, we know that we need to increase their facility with academic English. The new Common Core, Next Generation, and other state standards demand more rigorous use of language to express ideas, present arguments and counterclaims, justify one's reasoning, analyze material from several sources, and more. We advocate the inclusion of language objectives in all lessons as one significant means for teachers to help all students become better users of academic language.

As you plan your lessons, keep the following points in mind:

- Effective language objectives are aligned to the students' development needs and suited to the content topic being studied. They can be drawn from the texts students will read, the talk they will hear, the tasks they will be asked to perform, or the test they will be asked to take.

- Teachers need to understand the students' proficiency levels in order to select appropriate language objectives.

- All language objectives should include a specific language target that teachers will teach to and students will practice.

- Language objectives do not just reside on a whiteboard for display. They must be explicitly taught in a lesson, and students must be given opportunities to practice with the objectives.

- Language objectives are not written in differentiated statements. Differentiation occurs during the instruction and/or during practice and application activities.

Questions for Reflection

1. Which of the four categories of language objectives is the most challenging for you to incorporate into lessons? Why? What resources might you seek out and use to strengthen your skill set in that area?

2. Think about the most proficient readers in your class and the least proficient ones. Focusing on a specific literacy skill, how would you differentiate instruction for the group while keeping the same language objectives for all students in the class?

3. Sometimes teachers design objectives and post them without thinking through the instructional implications of those objectives. What lesson planning routine might assist you in making sure that the objectives are translated clearly into instruction?

4. Find a lesson that you taught in the past (or use a colleague's or find one online) that did not include a language objective. Write one for that lesson now. Review the plan and determine where you can insert some explicit instruction and practice to address that objective.

4

Building Academic Vocabulary

In this chapter you will

Content Objectives:

- Explore ways to select vocabulary words for explicit instruction
- Apply academic vocabulary techniques to your instruction

Language Objectives:

- Discuss word learning strategies
- Write activities that encourage development of word consciousness

In this chapter and the next, we explore two aspects of academic language that are critically important for English learners to acquire: vocabulary and oral language. These are two areas where English learners have a significant knowledge gap compared to English speakers because they did not grow up speaking and listening to English and learning words in English about the world around them. As the symbiotic nature of language development indicates, we know that when students strengthen their vocabulary and listening/speaking skills, their reading and writing abilities improve (August & Shanahan, 2008; Graves, 2006; Hiebert, & Kamil, 2005; Lesaux, Kieffer, Faller, & Kelley, 2010; Stahl & Nagy, 2005). Several studies have shown that teaching vocabulary can improve reading comprehension for both native English speakers (Beck, Perfetti, & McKeown, 1982) and English language learners (Carlo et al., 2004).

Academic Vocabulary Development

As we mentioned in Chapters 2 and 3, teachers typically feel comfortable teaching vocabulary. They may look for techniques to do it better or try more activities to move the definitions of words into students' long-term memory, but in general we do not have to sell the importance of vocabulary development to them. We can, however, offer suggestions for how to help English learners acquire the copious amount of words and concepts they need to be successful in school.

In Figure 4.1 we present five guidelines for vocabulary instruction. Drawn from research on vocabulary (Graves, 2006; Hiebert & Kamil, 2005; Lesaux, Kieffer, Faller, & Kelley, 2010; Nagy & Townsend, 2012; Stahl & Nagy, 2006, among others), they are not controversial; in fact they are common-sensical. They can be applied to any student, but we will describe some applications especially for students learning English as a new language.

Figure 4.1 Guidelines for Academic Vocabulary Instruction

1. Select words carefully and connect to the unit topic, theme, or essential question.
2. Teach words with visual supports, student-friendly examples, personal and bilingual connections.
3. Provide extensive practice with each key word.
4. Teach word learning strategies.
5. Develop word consciousness.

Word Selection

Draw from three categories of academic vocabulary. In our SIOP professional development work, we suggest teachers consider three categories when they select words for explicit instruction: (1) **key content and technical words**; (2) **general academic words** that include cross-curricular terms, process and function words, and logical connectors; and (3) **word parts** (Echevarria, Vogt, & Short, 2013).[1] The proportion of words drawn from these categories is likely to vary over the course of a unit, but some terms from all three should be addressed weekly.

The key content and technical terms will need to be taught so students learn the content topics and meet content standards. A number of these words, however, have limited use outside the classroom. Ask yourself when the last time was that you used the words *igneous* or *parabola*. You needed to know them when studying rocks or line graphs, and you learned them because they were critical to the lesson and used frequently in class. But it is unlikely they are part of your regular vocabulary outside of a school setting.

In contrast, when was the last time you used *conflict* or *analyze*? These more general academic terms have higher frequency of use inside, across, and outside classrooms. By teaching these terms to students, we are giving them words they can use in multiple subject areas. Some school systems ask teachers to introduce and reinforce these types of words

---

[1] Other researchers offer different categorizations of vocabulary terms. Beck, McKeown and Kucan (2002), for example, organize words into tiers. Tier 1 is basic words that the authors do not expect teachers to teach, such as *desk* and *rain* (although beginning English learners will need to be taught those words). Tier 2 is high-frequency words, akin to general academic terms as we define them here. Tier 3 is low-frequency words, often used for specific subjects.

across subjects and classes. So a middle school team of teachers, for example, may choose 20 such words, divide them up to teach but reinforce in all classes over two weeks, and then add another 20 for the next two weeks, and so on. An approach developed by Snow and colleagues, known as *Word Generation*, exemplifies this and has a growing research base (Snow, Lawrence, & White, 2009). An excellent resource for this category of academic vocabulary, particularly for secondary school, is the *Academic Word List* (Coxhead, 2000), which is available online and organizes approximately 3,000 words into 570 word families, known as *headwords*.[2]

Teaching word parts makes sense when you have examples in a text students will be reading and you can add other words with the same root, prefix, or suffix to the discussion. In a math lesson on angles, the word *bisect* may be taught. Teachers could also highlight the prefix *bi-* and have students learn its meaning; they then could teach or recall other words such as *bilateral, bicycle,* and *biweekly*. Word parts can also be taught through word study activities discussed later in this chapter.

Prioritize words for intensive instruction.   Knowing it is beneficial to select words from a range of categories is only a part of the lesson planning task. Prioritizing which words to teach explicitly is the next step. Often so many possibilities exist—especially for English learners who enter school with significant gaps in their vocabulary knowledge compared to English-speaking peers—that it is hard to narrow the list. Rarely can a teacher follow the same decision-making process for every lesson because a given unit will dictate how much emphasis needs to be placed on certain words. The decisions a teacher makes will therefore vary by lesson topic and by the lesson's placement within a unit. Technical and conceptual words likely need instruction in the first few lessons of a given unit, while academic terms and word parts may play a larger role in later lessons.

> ### Questions to Ask When Prioritizing Words for Intensive Instruction
>
> - *Is it a key word for the theme or unit topic?*
> - *Is it an academic word that will help students discuss, read, or write about the topic?*
> - *Is it a high-frequency word or of value beyond this lesson?*
> - *Is it a word that might confuse an English learner because it is similar to a known word, is a different meaning of a known word, or is idiomatic?*
> - *Do students have background knowledge about this topic already?*
> - *Is there an opportunity to teach a word part or a logical connector/transition word?*
> - *What is the proficiency level of my students and how might it affect my vocabulary decisions?*

Beck, McKeown and Kucan (2002, p. 19) suggest teachers consider the following when selecting words:

- **Importance and utility** (words that are highly useful and cross-curricular)
- **Instructional potential** (words that can be taught and practiced in various ways)
- **Conceptual understanding** (words for which students know the concept but not the more sophisticated word)

---

[2] One source listing all the words is http://www.uefap.com/vocab/select/awl.htm (at the time this book was written).

They also acknowledge some additional words will be required for comprehending a text, and thus they merit instruction, too.

Smith and Agnotti (2012) offer a tool, the *5 Cs* (Concepts, Content, Clarify, Cut, and Construct), for selecting words for a math lesson. We posit that the framework could be applied to any content area, and our discussion below puts their approach in the context of SIOP lessons.

1. **Concepts:** Determine which subject-specific or technical words are needed in the lesson.

2. **Content:** Determine which other general academic words are present in the lesson materials or are needed to discuss the topic or participate in lesson tasks.

3. **Clarify:** Identify words from the above two lists to briefly define, remind students of the definition, and clarify or paraphrase them when they appear in context. Teachers would not need to spend time on explicit instruction and practice. In a SIOP classroom, the clarification might occur through use of the students' native languages.

4. **Cut:** Identify words from the first two lists that do not need explanation. These might be words the teacher chooses not to use in teacher-crafted materials or words he or she will gloss over when they appear.

5. **Construct:** Decide which words to teach from the words remaining (i.e., those that do not appear on the lists created in steps 3 and 4).

A valuable contribution that Smith and Agnotti make in the fifth step is considering when to teach the words in a lesson. They point out that not all the words need to be taught up front, before a lesson starts. Some words may be taught during the lesson—specific to a task perhaps—and others taught at the end—after conceptual knowledge has been gained through activities. This corresponds to our point earlier that the time at which it is appropriate to teach words in a unit is variable as well. What Smith and Agnotti do not focus on are word parts, logical connectors, and transition words.

Find out what your students know. If you are an elementary classroom teacher or a secondary content teacher, you may want to consult with the ESL teacher who works with your students, especially if you have beginning and intermediate level students.[3] Do the students know common words already? Do they know prepositions and some conjunctions? There are several lists of high-frequency words that are useful guides in determining student knowledge, such as the top 1,000 words, the top 2,000 words, and the top 4,000 words. These can be found online. While these words, particularly the top 1,000, are more basic, everyday terms, knowing whether the students have knowledge of them can help teachers determine how they will explain their definitions and uses. Beyond the 2,000-word mark, teachers will find more words in the general academic category that are applicable to reading and discussion in their subjects. (A worthwhile resource is the *Text Project*, which has compiled several useful lists for teachers. The website at the time of this writing was http://textproject.org/teachers/word-lists/)

We suggest teachers brainstorm key words and potential words for an entire unit and then winnow the list down. Figure 4.2 on page 60 offers a chart to organize vocabulary selection and instruction. On page 61, we explain the categories along the top row of the chart.

---

[3] Some schools may not have an ESL or ELD teacher. In those cases, you might want to spend some time talking with your students, perhaps with small groups at lunchtime, to try and gauge their knowledge of basic English words.

Figure 4.2   Word Selection Chart

Unit Topic:			Unit Length:		
Category	Potential Words	Selected Words	When to Teach in the Unit	When to Teach in the Lesson	How to Teach	Practice Opportunities
Subject-specific					
General academic					
Word parts					

- **Potential Words:** Brainstorm all possible words in the three categories we recommend on page 57. Look at the instructional and assessment materials and consider the activities and resources students will use to accomplish lesson tasks and have academic conversations. Consider the proficiency level of the students and their background knowledge.

- **Selected Words:** Using your criteria (e.g., usefulness, relevance to topic, opportunity), narrow the potential list to a reasonable number of words to teach explicitly per lesson/week/unit. Some teachers use 10–12 words/week as a rule of thumb.
  - Don't forget the other potential words, however. Following Smith and Agnotti's advice, you may want to be prepared to briefly define, clarify, or rephrase these words if or when they come up in a lesson.

- **When to Teach in the Unit:** You may specify the lesson by its number in a unit, or simply note whether the words will be taught early, midway through, or late in the unit.

- **When to Teach in the Lesson:** Will you pre-teach the words early in the lesson? Teach them before reading a passage, or before students begin a task?

- **How to Teach:** Indicate how you will present new words to the students. Will you use visuals? Analogies? Demonstrations? Technology? Scenarios? Native language options? Will students try to determine the meaning themselves?

- **Practice Opportunities:** To the extent possible, identify several practice opportunities for the new words. The same opportunity may allow students to practice several words at once, for example, writing to a prompt using five words from a word bank or reading a passage with the words included. Ideally, at least one of the opportunities would compel students to generate or use the word on their own.

ACTIVITY

Practice selecting vocabulary words that you will teach. Fill in the chart in Figure 4.2. Consult the text you will be using and reflect on what you plan to say. Then, decide on which words to teach by using the *Questions to Ask When Prioritizing Words for Intensive Instruction* as a guide. Think about how you might teach those key words. For each word, ask yourself: *Does the meaning require a student-friendly definition? How will I connect the meaning to students' lives and prior knowledge? Is a video clip or visual needed to convey meaning? What graphic can I use to connect the word or word part to a larger unit?*

Word Instruction

Teachers have many resources at their disposal to engage students in vocabulary learning. Numerous books detail a wide range of activities for helping students learn and practice new words.[4] In our content books on the SIOP Model (Echevarria, Vogt & Short, 2010; Short, Vogt & Echevarria, 2011a; Short, Vogt & Echevarria, 2011b; Vogt, Echevarria, & Short, 2010), our contributors suggest specific techniques for teaching the vocabulary of mathematics, science, social studies, and English language arts. An increasing number of

---

[4] See, among others, Bear, et al., 2011; Beck, McKeown, & Kucan, 2002; Fisher & Frey, 2008; Graves, 2006; Graves, August, & Mancilla-Martinez, 2013; Marzano & Pickering, 2005; Vogt & Echevarria, 2008; Vogt, Echevarria, & Washam, 2014.

technological options exist as well. Online video clips, images, audio files, translation services, and more are at the teachers' and students' fingertips in many classrooms and can be used to convey word meanings. Silverman and Hines (2009) found that use of multimedia after reading to reinforce vocabulary led young English learners to statistically significant higher achievement compared to a control group of learners.

As you consult available books and draw from your own teaching experiences, we want to suggest you keep three things in mind: (1) consider each word in isolation so you convey its meaning effectively, (2) organize your lesson plans to include enough time for vocabulary instruction and practice, and (3) ensure your students record their new words in some form of vocabulary notebook.

Convey meaning effectively.　Teachers need to consider effective ways to build students' word knowledge when they provide explicit instruction of new words. Any technique used, such as those below, will likely necessitate some oral explanation by the teacher. It is important that those explanations are accompanied by student-friendly examples and, to the extent possible, connections to the students' personal lives, cultures, and/or prior learning. The meaning of the words in isolation is not the goal; how the words relate to or are used within the content topics being taught is.

- Some words will lend themselves to visual definition. Showing a picture, photo, or a real object can help students recognize the meaning of the word. These words are often concrete nouns and adjectives.

- The meanings of some abstract concepts or related words can be revealed through a video clip. Also, if students know the abstract concept in their native language, a quick translation may suffice.

- Some words, particularly verbs and some adverbs, can be demonstrated with physical movement (e.g., blink, to show *blink;* walk quickly then slowly to show *quickly* and *slowly*).

- Idioms can be difficult to teach because the meanings of the individual words that make up the idiom do not add up to the idiom's meaning. Idioms can be taught as lexical units (e.g., as a vocabulary phrase) with analogies and examples. (Idioms are further discussed in Chapter 7.)

- While we generally recommend putting to pasture the old standby "Look up the definitions in a dictionary and memorize them," if students have dictionary skills and a dictionary written for their proficiency level, they may look up words on their own to determine the meaning. Students may also be familiar with using handheld devices to find word meanings.

  For lower-level students, glossaries are typically better than dictionaries because the definitions provided are more targeted to the use of the words in that subject. (This is a problem with multiple-meaning words. Students may not know which meaning applies to the context in which they find the word.) Thesauri may also be consulted.

- Bilingual resources provide another way to convey meaning. Students may use electronic or paper bilingual dictionaries and electronic translation programs. Peers or the teacher may interpret a definition orally. Our goal is for students to understand the meaning of the new words and then be able to apply that meaning using English. So even if a student learns the definition of a word from a bilingual source, teachers will want students to practice using the word in English contexts.

- Connect words to the bigger picture, such as the theme or essential question. Don't assume students will make the association between words taught one day and those taught a few days later. Concept definition maps, semantic webs, annotated timelines, and other graphics can show the broad sweep of vocabulary in a unit.

> ### Ways to Teach New Words
>
> - *Pictures*
> - *Photos*
> - *Graphics*
> - *Pantomime and gestures*
> - *Video clips, multimedia*
> - *Dictionaries, thesauri*
> - *Glossaries*
> - *Bilingual tools (dictionaries, glossaries)*
> - *Bilingual oral definitions*
> - *Simulations and role plays*
> - *Songs and chants*

Some teachers like to have a routine or two for introducing new words. These routines have students think about the word no matter what method is used to initially convey the meaning. Students may be asked, for example, if the word is already familiar to them, or asked to rate its familiarity (e.g., show 1 finger if you know the word, show 2 fingers if it seems familiar, show 3 fingers if it is unknown). Students may be told the part of speech the word represents, and they may practice pronouncing the word. One of our valued SIOP colleagues, the late Liz Warner, suggested having students say the new words aloud in different ways—in a whisper, as a shout, robotically, fearfully, and so forth.

Some routines may be planned by the part of speech. For some action verbs, teachers may ask students to physically demonstrate or pantomime the word (e.g., twirl, walk with a limp, sow seeds). For some nouns and adjectives, students may be asked to draw a picture. For some words, the teacher may say, "Show Me . . ." (focus on adjectives: a sad face, something purple, an evil eye, something smaller than a ruler) or "Tell Me Someone Who . . ." (focus on nouns: is a politician, works with animals).

Routines also may involve more cognitive demand than recall or comprehension. Students can make an original sentence with one word or more than one word, write definitions or original sentences in their own language, and/or note synonyms or antonyms.

Organize instructional time. Another consideration when planning vocabulary instruction is deciding the amount of time to spend on the words in one lesson or across lessons. Lessons early in a unit may merit more time spent on vocabulary than those that occur later because students must learn new concept words and additional words (e.g., general academic terms) that will allow them to talk about the topic right away. More repetition will be needed initially, too, as students are acquiring the new words, than later when they can recall the words with ease. Over the course of the unit, the number of new words that require explicit instruction may diminish, as shown in this illustration.

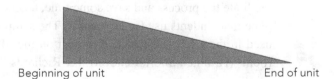

Beginning of unit   End of unit

It is also possible that the vocabulary instruction may ebb and flow as in the second illustration, below. In a unit that includes two related readings, for example, new words may need to be taught in advance of each passage.

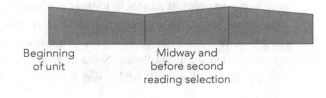

Beginning
of unit   Midway and
before second
reading selection

Within a lesson, vocabulary instruction typically happens at the beginning, but that need not be the case all the time. A teacher may prepare a hands-on discovery activity for students to do and then introduce vocabulary afterwards as they talk about the experience. Students at advanced proficiency levels may engage in a technique called *Vocabulary Self-Collection Strategy (VSS)* in which they identify words they think are important to learn from a reading, for instance, develop a class list, and find the meanings (Ruddell & Shearer, 2002).

In some cases, as explained earlier, the teacher may decide not to spend time teaching all the new words, especially those deemed less important. However, he or she may provide an adjunct glossary, a study guide, or use the glosses that appear at the bottom of pages in many student materials published in recent years that quickly give meanings to students and allow them to move on with a reading or an activity. In approaches like *Text Talk* (Beck, McKeown, & Kucan, 2002) for young learners, teachers stop and clarify words as they read text aloud and engage students briefly in discussions of the words' meanings. Our colleagues working on Project QuEST in the CREATE research program used a specific routine to pre-teach key science vocabulary in classes with English and Spanish speakers (August, Artzi & Mazrum, 2010). Teachers used a card with two pictures (one on the front, another on the back) representing a key word. When showing one picture to the class, the teacher provided English and Spanish definitions, indicated if the word were a cognate, and explained the word's application to the science concept that would be taught. When shown the second picture, partners were asked to tell each other how the picture related to the meaning of the term.

> **ACTIVITY**
>
> Look at a text passage that you or your students will read aloud. Identify words that you will not pre-teach but that you may need to clarify. Plan how you will do so while the reading process takes place.

Have students keep vocabulary notebooks. It is critically important for English learners to record new words as they learn them. In some schools, note-taking has lost its significance, but English learners need to have a dedicated portion of their class notebook or a separate "personal dictionary" or "word study book" in which to write down the word and its meaning as well as any other memory devices they choose (as noted above, drawing a picture, writing an original sentence, etc.). The process of writing the word down and adding meaningful notes helps students remember the word and take some ownership over it.

deep processing

Because this is an important task, as teachers plan their lessons, they need to adjust the pacing to ensure time for recording vocabulary. The investment in time is worthwhile because students will have a tangible product that they can refer to, add to, and review. To facilitate the process and save some time, teachers might want to develop a vocabulary template that students use for key words. The sample in Figure 4.3 is based on the template we used in the CREATE research project on the SIOP Model in middle school science classrooms (Himmel, Short, Echevarria & Richards-Tutor, 2012).

Extensive Word Practice

A critical point to remember is that teaching a new word to students is not sufficient for them to learn the word. Researchers suggest that students need 12–15 meaningful exposures to new words in order to add them to their academic repertoire (Nagy & Anderson, 1984). This means that we cannot expect students to learn new words and be able to use them without support after a one-time introduction. Nor can we show them a flash card or point 12 times to a word posted on a word wall. Some high-frequency words that are also concrete, such as *pen*, *book*, and *desk*, will be learned fairly easily, but others, such as *osmosis*, *theme*, and

Figure 4.3 **Vocabulary Notebook Template**

Vocabulary Strategy Checklist

Word	Definition
Part of speech	

Check the box of the strategy you will use to remember the word.

- ☐ Imagery (draw a picture)
- ☐ Spider Map (body is the word, details and examples are the legs)
- ☐ Synonym and antonym
- ☐ Context (use the word in an original sentence)
- ☐ 4-corner chart
- ☐ Frayer Map
- ☐ Native language definition
- ☐ Concept definition map

In the box below, show how you are using this strategy.

factor, will indeed require more repetition and in-depth practice (Fukkink, & de Glopper, 1998). The next section provides ideas for creating meaningful exposures to new words.

Practice. Providing time for students to practice using the new academic language they are acquiring is critical to the learning process. English learners require repetition to obtain and retain new vocabulary and sentence structures. Practice and repetition also allow students to produce more language and use it in the different ways required in school settings.

Practice opportunities vary by lesson and topic. It is important not only to convey the meaning of words but also to explore with students how they are used. In some cases, for instance, this process may involve distinguishing among denotation, connotation, figurative language use, and multiple meanings (as called for in the Common Core English language arts standards). Since adequate reading comprehension depends on a person already knowing 90%–95% of the words in a text read independently (Nagy & Scott, 2000), we have to work to get vocabulary into the students' mental toolbox.

On days that teachers introduce new words, they should have some activities prepared for students to use the words. These may include activities related to recording the words in a vocabulary notebook or reading a text with the new words and discussing them as part of a reading comprehension check. On subsequent days, teachers should have students work with the words through all four language domains. Ideas that can be explored over time include creating concept maps that link words thematically, using the words in oral skits and writing assignments, noticing the words in other contexts (e.g., the textbook of another subject, song lyrics), and combining words in responses to questions. The goal of this "word work" is to deepen the students' understanding of the word and to consider how known words relate to new words. It can also help students consider multiple-meaning words (e.g., How does *power* as used in science class differ from *power* in math class?) and idioms.

To obtain a clearer picture of how a teacher can go beyond a word and its definition, see the sample activities shown in Figure 4.4. (Chapter 7 discusses this topic in more depth.)

A good rule of thumb is to get students back into their vocabulary notebooks several times a week. Have the English learners recognize the notebooks for the resources they can be. Students can add to words already there by noting related words or providing more examples.

Figure 4.4 **Sample Activities to Deepen Vocabulary Knowledge**

Activities to Deepen Vocabulary Knowledge

Activities	Task
Idea Completion (Beck, McKeown & Kucan, 2002)	Provide a sentence starter for students to complete, such as "When I feel *conflicted*, I ____."
Word Relationships (Beck, McKeown & Kucan, 2002)	Set up reasonable or unreasonable relationships between two words and have students respond. For example, "Could a *patriot* be a *traitor*?"
Have You Ever . . .? (Beck, McKeown & Kucan, 2002)	Personalize the word for students to respond to questions like "Have you ever seen a *glacier*? and "Would you ever *break a promise*?"
Word Associations (Beck, McKeown & Kucan, 2002)	Ask students to recall/find a word that goes with a given word and explain the connection.
Word Sorts (Bear, et al., 2011)	Have students sort a set of terms according to predetermined categories or their own categories.
List-Group-Label (Readance, Bean, & Baldwin, 2012)	In this variation of Word Sort, first, have students generate words related to a topic (list). Second, ask them to look at the words and try to arrange them in groups (group). Third, have them provide a category name for the groups they have established (label).
Word Hunt	Give students a list of words with multiple meanings. Have them identify one meaning they know, find another meaning, record an example in print or online, and write an original sentence with the new meaning.

Set daily vocabulary routines. We recommend that teachers set aside time daily to work with vocabulary, maybe taking 5 minutes at the beginning or end of class to review words through a quick-write prompt or a vocabulary game. Instead of telling students that they can start their homework when the class finishes early, play a vocabulary game like bingo, Pictionary, Concentration, mix & match, or word splash. When students finish reading a passage and working on comprehension activities, they can go back into the text and look for cognates, root words, words related to a predetermined term, and so forth.

Word Learning Strategies

It is said that students who do the best academically know the most words. And some research bears this out, particularly when academic achievement is measured by standardized tests (Blachowicz, Fisher, Ogle, & Watts-Taffe, 2006; Stanovich, 1986). Why is this so? Knowing the meaning of words makes reading more pleasurable, which leads to more time spent reading. More time spent reading results in exposure to more words and increased vocabulary. When reading is difficult, it is typically avoided, which reduces a student's exposure to words.

Consider this: if you know more words, you typically know more concepts. If you know higher-level categories (i.e., concepts), you have schema upon which to add new words as you learn them. If you organize words by association, when asked about one word in a category, you may remember other related words. Now think about standardized tests that students take. Often the correct answer among multiple-choice options includes a synonym or word related to a key word in the question. Further, writing tasks scored by a rubric often are judged in part by traits such as word choice and development of ideas—traits that rely on vocabulary knowledge. This reflection on academic performance leads us to conclude that it is important for students to develop robust vocabularies.

It has been reported that native English speakers who enter school at age 5 or 6 typically have a spoken vocabulary of 6,000 words (Resnick & Snow, 2009). As we noted in Chapter 2, native English speakers are expected to have a reading vocabulary[5] of 25,000 word families by the end of 8th grade; and by the end of high school, students who plan a post-secondary career should have a reading vocabulary of 50,000 word families (Graves, 2006). How can our students learn this many words?

Think about your instruction. How many words do you teach each week on average in one class? To meet the benchmarks mentioned above, students need to learn 3,000 words or more per year in school. However, direct instruction of words in class never reaches that number. So students must learn words on their own. Some learning occurs through interaction with peers (e.g., new terms describing music and fashion, slang words) and incidental learning (e.g., when told to *ladle* some soup into a bowl, a child may learn both what a ladle is and how to ladle). The type of words learned in this way may be less academic than is needed at school.

Teach strategies to learn new words.   The best way to move students toward the 50,000-word goal by the end of 12th grade is by teaching them how to learn new words. The third category for word selection that we discussed earlier—word parts—applies here. Some of the strategic instruction students need to begin learning words on their own comes from helping them parse words by looking for familiar affixes and roots. They should also learn to look for cognates and to examine the context of a new word in a text. Individual choice to consult an electronic or print dictionary or a more knowledgeable person is still another way to learn new words.

- **Prefixes and suffixes.** It is valuable to teach the most common prefixes and suffixes so students can apply their meaning to unfamiliar words that contain an affix. The top 20 prefixes account for 97% of the prefixed words that appear in printed school

---

[5] For most people their speaking vocabulary—words they produce—is smaller than their reading vocabulary—words they recognize in print or in conversation.

English, and the percentage is similar for suffixes. The top 9 prefixes and suffixes account for approximately 70%. A teacher can choose to focus on one affix every week or so, and over the course of one school year can provide students with some effective tools for determining the meaning of words on their own. In one study, 3rd graders who were taught the top 9 and a strategy for breaking words into roots and suffixes outperformed a control group on several measures of word meaning (White, Sowell, & Yanagihara, 1989).

- **Roots and base words.** As with the affixes, investing the time to teach students the common roots of academic terms can yield a payoff in determining the meaning of new words. Many of the roots of words in secondary school math and science textbooks, for example, have origins in Latin or Greek, so students whose first language is based on either one have an advantage in figuring out the meanings. Similarly, students can examine a word for a familiar base word (e.g., *care, careful, careless, childcare, Medicare*).

  Once students know affixes, roots, and bases, they can begin to apply morphemic knowledge (i.e., knowledge of word parts) to new words. They can create new words and try to determine the meaning of unknown words.

- **Cognates.** Effective language learners make use of their native language and literacy skills. Looking for cognates is one key strategy (Dressler, Carlo, Snow, August, & White, 2011). Sometimes the cognate of the academic term is used more frequently in the native language than in English. For example, in everyday language we often use *speed* but in physics class we use *velocity*. In Spanish, *velocidad* is the common term, both as everyday language and as school language. Cognates may be recognized for the full word or for the root or an affix. (See Lubliner & Hiebert, 2011 for an analysis of Spanish–English cognates that appear on the *Academic Word List*.)

- **Context.** In many classrooms we hear teachers tell students to figure out the meaning of a word by rereading and looking for clues in nearby words in a sentence. This strategy is not helpful if there are several other words in the sentence that students do not know, as can often be the case for students at lower proficiency levels. When a text is near their reading level, this strategy might work, especially if students learn to look at graphics that complement the text as well. But for more difficult texts, other strategies are needed.

  o One suggestion is the strategy of "guess and replace." Tell students to guess what they think the word means, replace the unknown word with the guess in the sentence, and then read on and see if it makes sense.

  o Another is simply to read on. Sometimes the word is defined in the next sentence, an example is provided, or its meaning otherwise becomes clearer. (Conversely, one might need to read back. A prior sentence or paragraph might signal the meaning.)

- **Syntax/Sentence Structure.** Students can also be taught to determine the role of the word in a sentence (e.g., its part of speech) and/or its position. What part of speech is the unknown word? Does it seem to be the verb of the sentence? Is it accompanied by a familiar adverb? Does it occur after the word *the*? If so, it must be a noun or adjective modifying a noun. Does it occur after the word *in*? Then it could be an adjective, adverb, noun, or gerund. In either case, it would never be a verb. Students can also notice if there is an appositive after the word, a phrase set off by commas or dashes that defines the new word.

Teachers can instruct students on all of these strategies through modeling and think-alouds. Focusing in on one paragraph or one sentence, using a smartboard, document reader, or even an overhead projector, and talking through the application of one or more of these strategies will demonstrate to students how these mental tools can help them make meaning.

Promote incidental learning.   We learn many words incidentally through listening and reading by means of visual and oral contextual clues (Cunningham, 2005). English learners, however, might learn fewer words this way because the contextual words that scaffold meaning to a new word may be unknown as well. Also, unfortunately, many English learners come from low socioeconomic households where their families do not regularly participate in literacy activities like those performed in school (Garcia, 2001). Therefore, they may not have easy access to a resource (e.g., when reading outside of school) to consult on the meaning of an unknown word. This reality places the onus on teachers to organize opportunities for English learners to engage with text (oral and written, online or in print) for pleasure and to interact with native English speakers or advanced English learners as another means for practicing and learning words.

Word Consciousness

We want students to be aware of words as they read and listen and to consider their choice of words as they write and speak. When students become more aware of words, it increases their incidental learning, too. As Graves, August, & Mancilla-Martinez (2013) point out, word consciousness encompasses cognitive and affective mindsets. We encourage students to pay attention to words, look for relationships and nuances among words (e.g., synonyms, antonyms), recognize formal and informal discourse, and actively seek to learn more words (Scott & Nagy, 2004). We also want them to have fun with words, comprehend jokes and puns, and use idioms appropriately. Finally, we want them to call on and apply the linguistic knowledge they have acquired in their native language. By helping English learners develop this awareness and these skills, we enable them to become more independent learners and move them toward proficiency in academic English.

The following ideas may be useful pursuits toward the goal of word consciousness:

- Novice learners can find words they know in texts and words that look familiar but for which they are unsure of the meaning. They can copy them on a T-chart to distinguish the known and the familiar. This activity is sometimes used in learning stations during guided reading time.

- All learners can collect words they do not know. Some teachers designate one day of the week as Word Detective Day; they invite students to bring in one word they would like to learn and ask them to describe the context in which they found the word. The class then tries to determine the word's meaning.

- Students can maintain personal dictionaries in either hard copy, electronic copy, or online. An electronic personal dictionary has several benefits: students can add images to their words and definitions; they can easily add more information as they learn about a word or change information as they clarify meaning; and they enjoy using the technology.

- Given that English has many multiple-meaning words, students should learn to test their assumptions. In other words, when they see a word whose meaning they know (e.g., *table* as in table and chairs), they should check whether the meaning applies in the context they encounter (e.g., a *table* displaying data). Parent (2009) offers some pedagogical suggestions for addressing these types of words.

- In some classes, teachers ask students to set word learning goals; for example, "I will learn 10 new words on my own this month." Teachers periodically check in with the students and plan time for them to share their new words with a partner or in a small group.

- As in the children's book *Miss Alaineous* (Frazier, 2007), a class or a school can hold a Vocabulary Parade. Students choose one word and dress up in a costume that represents that word. The class or school holds the parade. If the parade is videotaped, an ideal follow-up is for the students to view and count how many words they know and look for new ones to learn.

- More advanced students can start to consider collocations and other fixed expressions. Collocations are words that typically appear together, more frequently than by chance. We may say *head wound* or *head injury*, for example, but while we say *spinal injury* we do not say *spinal wound*. Also, we use many fixed phrases like *as a result* and *in conclusion* in academic text and discussions. Students benefit from explicit instruction in these fixed expressions and are more likely to retain them when they are taught as such. (See Chapter 7 for more information.)

- Teachers often express frustration at overused words, such as *fine* and *interesting*, in student writing. Two techniques that help students with word choice are *Rest-in-Peace (RIP)* and *Shooting Star*s.

  - *RIP words:* The class agrees to put overused words to rest. Students cut out headstone shapes,[6] list words on them, and post them in the classroom.

  - *Shooting Star words:* Students select more sophisticated words, such as synonyms, to replace RIP words. They cut out star shapes, list words on them, and post them in the classroom, ideally next to each RIP word.

- When possible, teachers can concretize figurative language to help students distinguish among that type of language, straightforward definitions (denotations), and associated definitions (connotations). For example, one of our original SIOP teacher-researchers, Barbara Formoso, developed a lesson on similes and metaphors with household objects (e.g., stapler, crazy straw, spaghetti tongs). She asked students to complete a T-chart. First, she showed each item to students in the regular classroom lighting. Students recorded what each item was and wrote a literal description of it. Then she asked them to imagine each item as something else or for another use. To help, she turned off the light, and, using a flashlight, cast a shadow on each object for students to see. Students recorded their imagined objects in the next column along with a sentence for each using the new description. Then the class applied this knowledge to literal and figurative interpretations of a Langston Hughes poem.

ACTIVITY

Think about an academic vocabulary success your students experienced in this past year. Write a brief description of the lesson(s) you planned and the vocabulary development the students underwent.

---

[6] If headstones are culturally inappropriate for some of your students, cut out circle shapes, list the words, and draw a red diagonal line across the circle.

Application to Common Core Standards

The instruction of academic vocabulary is directly applicable to the Common Core standards for English language arts and also is important for students to meet the Common Core mathematics and Next Generation science standards. Academic vocabulary is referenced in the standards of non-CCSS states as well. Let's look at ELA Anchor Standard 4 for Reading, which is the same for all grades K–12:

- Interpret words and phrases as they are used in a text, including determining technical, connotative, and figurative meanings, and analyze how specific word choices shape meaning or tone.

We see that in order to meet this standard, teachers must carefully select words that have "technical, connotative, and figurative meanings" and teach them. Further, for students to comprehend reading passages with these words, they need to have practice opportunities to learn them and analyze their meanings when used in text. The focus on these types of meanings as well as "specific word choices" taps into developing students' word consciousness.

Vocabulary acquisition and use is the focus of three Anchor Standards for Language in the CCSS English Language Arts (#4, 5, and 6):

- Determine or clarify the meaning of unknown and multiple-meaning words and phrases by using context clues, analyzing meaningful word parts, and consulting general and specialized reference materials, as appropriate.
- Demonstrate understanding of figurative language, word relationships, and nuances in word meanings.
- Acquire and use accurately a range of general academic and domain-specific words and phrases sufficient for reading, writing, speaking, and listening at the college and career readiness level; demonstrate independence in gathering vocabulary knowledge when encountering an unknown term important to comprehension or expression.

As with the reading standard, the importance of careful word selection for general academic and content-specific words is evident, as is the need for fostering word consciousness, which includes not only knowing about words and their meanings but also adding words to one's academic repertoire. The application of vocabulary to reading, writing, listening, and speaking tasks is clear and the development of word learning strategies is called for.

Within the SIOP Model we have multiple opportunities to address vocabulary in ways that will help students meet these standards. As we have noted elsewhere, teachers may make vocabulary a *language objective* (Feature 2) for a lesson. This would mean that they plan for some *explicit instruction on key words* (or a word part) (Feature 9), provide *supplementary materials* as needed (e.g., photos, video clips) (Feature 4), and follow through with *meaningful practice or application activities* (Features 6, 20, 21, 24) as the lesson unfolds. They may focus on *word learning strategies* (Feature 13). At the end of the lesson, they would *review the key words* too (Feature 27).

Even when vocabulary is not a focus of the language objective (LO), it is highlighted in SIOP lessons. We expect some *vocabulary teaching or review* in most SIOP lessons (Feature 9), and the other building background features (Features 7, 8)—*connections to students' background experiences and prior learning*—necessitate the activation or construction of key concepts, which will involve discussion of related terms. At times, during academic discussions or while students are reading, the teacher may need to *clarify a term in the native language*

(Feature 19). One would also expect that the practice and application activities and higher-order thinking tasks, even when vocabulary is not the focus of the LO, would engage students in using and applying the content-specific words and general academic terms.

Let's think through what a SIOP lesson might be like. Suppose the subject was U.S. Government and the topic was how legislation becomes a law. This lesson is part of a unit on the Congress, and students have studied the structure of the two houses and their constitutional functions. The content objective is

> ...ents will explain the steps for a bill to become a law.

The language objective is

> Students will determine the meaning of new words using roots, suffixes, and graphic clues.

The language objective is derived from the ELA Anchor Standard 4 for Language discussed above.

The teacher begins by tapping prior learning, asking half of the student groups to list functions of the House of Representatives and the other half, functions of the Senate. After the groups have brainstormed their lists, the class creates a Venn diagram. The students take turns offering ideas for the three sections of the Venn diagram. If the class agrees to an idea, that student writes the function he or she presented on the smartboard. The teacher weighs in as needed.

The teacher then uses the information in the Venn diagram to pre-teach key words for a reading on the legislative process: *policy, bill, majority,* and *debate.* Students record the words in their vocabulary notebooks using the vocabulary strategy template (as shown in Figure 4.3), and the teacher plans for students to determine the meaning of the following as they conduct the informational reading: *legislation, compromise, veto,* and *amend.* He reminds the students of learning strategies they can use to determine the meaning of new words:

- Look at the word and determine if you know it or if it is familiar. If it is familiar, take a guess at the meaning. Does the guess make sense in the sentence?
- Look for a prefix, suffix, root, or base word you know. Does that help you find the meaning?
- Look for a cognate.
- Look at the graphics.

The students then read the pages in the textbook on the legislative process. When done, in small groups, they discuss the gist of the process and possible definitions for the selected words. As a class, they then review the new words' meanings and students add them to their notebooks.

To check on student understanding of the steps, the teacher then distributes sentence strips that summarize the process of how a bill becomes law, one strip per student pair. The pair is asked to find where their summary statement fits into the text they read and then are to read a few sentences or paragraphs, before and after, so they recognize their place in the process[7]. The student pairs then physically get in order at the front of the room holding their sentence strips. The teacher asks the pairs to read and explain their steps in order.

---

[7] Our thanks to Carola Osses, an ESL teacher at Norwalk High School, Norwalk, CT, for suggesting this extra step in a sentence strip activity.

At the end of the class, students share one thing they learned that day in their groups and the teacher reviews the objectives and new vocabulary.

Summary

Many of the practices we advocate in this chapter will enable students to meet the English language arts and literacy standards defined in the Common Core and in other state standards. Deeper knowledge of vocabulary will help them in other subject areas as well. One critical responsibility we have as educators is to help students access the meaning of words and the connections among words, whether through direct instruction, use of vocabulary strategies, or incidental learning. Keep the following points in mind as you plan your instruction:

- Students with rich, robust vocabularies perform well in school, which is why we need to increase vocabulary instruction for English learners.
- Words must be carefully selected for instruction and should include content-specific and general academic words as well as word parts.
- Students need extensive practice and exposure to new words in multiple contexts. Practice should involve all four language skills.
- Students benefit from instruction in word learning strategies and encouragement to develop word consciousness.
- Explicit instruction of key words is critical, but students also need to learn hundreds of words through incidental learning both inside and outside of the classroom.
- Vocabulary knowledge is an important part of the Common Core State Standards for English language arts. The SIOP Model offers an instructional approach for meeting those goals.

Questions for Reflection

1. Think about the way you typically select key words for instructional purposes. How does it differ from the process presented in this chapter? What specifically will you alter about the process you typically use?

2. Encouraging students to be aware of words as they read and listen contributes to the likelihood that they will add new words to their vocabulary repertoire. What are some word consciousness practices listed on pp. 69–70 that you will implement in lessons? Are there any others that you might add to the list?

3. A number of word learning strategies are presented in this chapter. Which do you think would present the greatest challenge for English learners? Why? Which might be the easiest? Why?

4. Consider your state standards for English language arts and other subjects. Which standards focus on vocabulary? Explain how using the SIOP Model can help you plan lessons so students can meet those standards.

5. A number of vocabulary techniques were described in this chapter. Find one that is new to you, or a modification of one you know, and describe how you might use it in a lesson.

5 Enhancing Academic Oral Language

Fotolia

In this chapter you will

Content Objectives:

- Explain how oral language development relates to the Common Core State Standards or other state standards
- Apply oral language activities to your classroom

Language Objectives:

- Rewrite a lesson plan for beginning English learners that provides oral language practice
- Read and summarize the guidelines for effective oral language development

As we noted in Chapter 4, most English learners enter U.S. schools with weaker oral language skills than native English speakers. They have had much less exposure to the sounds, words, and phrases of English than their native-speaking peers and far fewer opportunities to develop an innate sense of English grammar. So, as with vocabulary development, teachers need to help these learners catch up. To do so, teachers must provide explicit instruction in listening and speaking skills and create classroom environments that invite collaborative academic discussions. Passive learning, that is, sitting quietly while listening to a teacher talk, happens far too often in our schools, and it does not encourage engagement or discussion. It may offer listening practice (if the students know how to listen to lectures and mini-presentations in ways that they can acquire knowledge), but in order to acquire academic oral language, students must be offered lessons that are meaningful and engaging and provided with ample opportunity to practice using English orally.

We cannot rely exclusively upon the strategy of questioning as a tool to promote classroom talk. Researchers have found that explicit, "right there" questions—basic recall questions or questions with answers easily found in text—are used between 50% and 80% of the time in classrooms (Watson & Young, 1986; Zwiers, 2008). These questions serve primarily one purpose—to determine student comprehension about concrete and literal information. In contrast, effective instructional practices for classroom talk focus very seriously on dialogue to promote learning; it is the back and forth discussion that fosters critical thinking, develops verbal reasoning skills, and builds background knowledge.

Part of the challenge for teachers is not only to plan meaningful activities but also to group students so their discussions have value and purpose. For pair and group work to be successful, teachers must demonstrate to students how to work with others effectively, how to take turns in discussions and build on other's ideas, and how to move forward collaboratively to reach the intended outcome of the task.

Instruction should connect the topic to the students' personal lives and background knowledge and promote academic talk that is collaborative in nature. In many lessons, students have to take a stance and debate a point of view, participate in a role-play, or do some research as part of a collaborative project and report out to their peers as experts. In each one of these structured opportunities to talk, students can learn from their peers by observing and listening, and they can be tasked with using specialized language registers, grammatical structures, and vocabulary words to improve their academic language skills.

Academic Oral Language Development

It has been said that speaking is the neglected language standard and listening is the forgotten one, but long before the Common Core put speaking and listening on almost equal status with reading and writing, our work with the SIOP Model showed teachers how to design lessons that build oral discourse skills among English learners and use oral language as a tool to support and strengthen other literacy skills. If the English/language arts standards call for more language development, if the math and science standards want more communication and justification, and if the other content classes promote more literacy, the SIOP Model supports these efforts. SIOP teachers design lessons that enable students to work on all four language skills across the content areas.

Research has shown that English learners benefit from the integration of explicit instruction in reading, writing, listening, and speaking across the curriculum, regardless of their proficiency level (Genesee et al., 2006; Saunders & O'Brien, 2006). These skills are mutually reinforcing domains, even though students do not always make progress at the same rate in each domain (August & Shanahan, 2006; Echevarria, Short, & Powers, 2006). We argue that to become proficient in academic language, students must be able to participate actively in the oral discourse of the classroom as well as the reading and writing tasks.

In Figure 5.1 we present seven guidelines for academic oral language instruction.

Figure 5.1 Guidelines for Academic Oral Language Instruction

1. Establish a classroom environment that promotes rich discussion.
2. Give students something interesting to talk about.
3. Teach active listening.
4. Scaffold structures so students can express their ideas with appropriate language functions.
5. Demonstrate language models.
6. Provide multiple opportunities to practice.
7. Talk less.

A Positive, Respectful, and Communal Classroom Environment

Establishing a classroom environment that feels safe and respectful to English learners is one key to promoting oral language development. Many people need to feel comfortable before they are willing to speak with others, especially in a group setting. This is all the more true for English learners, if they are to take risks using their new language and practicing the oral language functions desired. The teacher sets the stage by expressing acceptance of individual differences, by welcoming all attempts to use the new language, by encouraging students to support their peers and build on their ideas, and by correcting errors during discussion only as needed to avoid confusion. The teacher must change the typical dynamic in class where teachers talk 80% of the time and allow the time for more student-centered, academic conversations to take place.

A number of researchers have pointed out the sociocultural aspect of classroom participation, which goes beyond just knowing the content and academic vocabulary (Cook-Gumperz, 2006; Gallimore & Tharp,1988; Gillanders, Castro, & Franco, 2014; Moschkovich, 2007). It includes the social contexts in which discussions take place; the power relationships among the speakers; the cultural relevancy of the topic; and the gestures, symbols, and other non-verbal communication practices. These aspects of the classroom dynamic affect student engagement and can encourage or discourage student participation. Our goal as effective teachers is to create a classroom culture that values the contributions of all students (in English and the students' native languages) and fosters the co-construction of knowledge between the teacher and learners.

A positive and supportive environment also involves the classroom set-up. Student desks should be in clusters so discussion can occur easily. Environmental print on the walls can support discussions with charts of signal words, sentence starters, concept maps, and vocabulary. Providing students access to on-level reading materials and technology (e.g., a bank of computers) is important if they are to do some research and report back. Having space in the room for students to stand and move around so they can speak with multiple partners or chart information on walls in small groups is also beneficial to interaction.

Interesting Topics for Discussion

If we want students to talk, we need to give them something interesting to talk about. While planning lessons, teachers should ask themselves: What would make a topic interesting?

Choose grade-level topics.   First, we would want the topic to be appropriate to students' grade-level curriculum so they are exposed to key topics that their peers are studying. Such exposure will be more motivating to the students, particularly adolescents who will recognize the relevance of the material (Short & Fitzsimmons, 2007). Even beginners can be introduced to key topics in their English as a second language (ESL) classes so they gain access to the core curriculum.

Link topics to a theme or essential question.   Second, we suggest the discussions be linked to a bigger unit theme or essential question. A thematic approach helps students integrate language and content learning and develop what they know over time. As students learn key vocabulary words, they can use them orally in structured activities and add new related words to their repertoire as their study of the theme progresses. As they gain more knowledge about the theme, they can apply it in different ways to practice different language functions. For example, students may begin a study of rocks and address the question "How Do Rocks Differ?" in discussion over several days by *describing* characteristics of different rocks, *comparing* different types of rocks, and then analyzing mystery samples to *express observations* and *draw conclusions* in order to determine the types of rocks in the samples. Essential questions can engage and motivate students to explore and share possible answers. By building vocabulary, listening skills, and speaking skills in context during the course of a thematic unit, students can respond more thoughtfully to the essential question, building on their own ideas and those of their peers as they gain new perspectives, information, and data.

Tap personal connections and background experiences. Third, we suggest that teachers tap into the students' personal connections to the topic of study (Gillanders, et al, 2014; Moje, et al., 2004). Such discussions may take place while activating or building background knowledge of a topic or may occur as the result of reading a particular text passage. With teacher facilitation, students can use their oral language skills to access and share their prior content knowledge. Techniques for this include:

- Show a picture, real object, or video clip to generate a discussion. (What do you see? Does it remind you of anything? Have you ever been to this place? How does it relate to our topic?)

- Set up a hands-on discovery activity related to the topic and have students orally retell what they did and/or concluded (e.g., use magnets to try to move objects made of different materials).

- Encourage students to talk about a new topic in their native language if a classmate speaks the language too. They could then try to summarize the discussion in English, draw a picture to represent the connection, or act it out.

All of these ideas can be adjusted to request that students use certain words, phrases, or language frames as they discuss their connections. These structured opportunities are explained in more detail below.

Invite opinions and perspectives. Fourth, we have found that students are often motivated to participate in a discussion when their viewpoints or opinions are solicited or they are asked to make a prediction, evaluation, or speculation. This calls for some critical and/or creative thinking too.

- **Take a Stand**—Mark the four corners of the classroom as follows: Strongly Agree, Agree, Disagree, and Strongly Disagree. Read statements to the students related to the upcoming lesson topic (e.g., "High school students should have an 11 p.m. curfew on school nights." "The world should stop using nuclear power plants."). The students move to the corner that represents their view. They discuss their ideas in small groups and choose one person to report out their position on the issue. After hearing all the positions, students have an opportunity to move to a different corner if their viewpoint changed.

- **Anticipation Guides**—As an anticipatory activity, these guides can spark students' interest at the start of a unit or lesson, or before reading a text or viewing a video clip. Ask students their opinions on a topic, have them predict the results of some

Figure 5.2 **Anticipation Guide for *Macbeth***

1. The three witches put a curse on Macbeth's enemies to aid him.	True	False
2. Lady Macbeth kills King Duncan so her husband will become king.	True	False
3. Lady Macbeth feels guilty and kills herself.	True	False
4. King Duncan's son will avenge his murder.	True	False

experiments, or have them guess information that is included in a text or the outcome of a story. Write 3 to 5 statements using a simple response format: Agree or Disagree, Yes or No, True or False, or use a Likert scale. Figure 5.2 is an example.

Active Listening

To foster effective verbal interaction, teachers need to teach students how to become active listeners. Although hearing is more of a physical phenomenon (registering sound vibrations), listening is a complex cognitive process that involves knowledge of the sound system, vocabulary, syntax, nonverbal cues, and pragmatics. Listening is also influenced by knowledge of the topic; it is less cognitively demanding to listen to input about something familiar than something new or complicated. Listening may be unidirectional (no response to what is heard is expected) or bidirectional (the give and take of a conversation). Both types occur in classroom contexts.

English learners need deliberate instruction to develop strong listening comprehension skills in their new language (Ashcraft & Tran, 2010; Hinkel, 2006; Saunders & Goldenberg, 2010). One way to do this is by teaching note-taking skills. When we combine note-taking with listening, we can show students how to recognize speech cues (e.g., ways that teachers indicate important points, such as with key phrases, voice inflection, and repetition) so they can record the critical information instead of trying to copy down everything that a teacher is saying. This means they also learn to ignore some information. We should explain that typically in school we listen for a purpose, and if that purpose is articulated ahead of time, it is easier to focus on the information being shared. It is also beneficial to teach students how to use abbreviations. If we add some reflection time after the note-taking, students can learn to categorize and summarize their notes, which will help them in reviewing information later.

The following three techniques demonstrate ways to promote academic listening:

- **Dictoglos**—One common listening technique is dictation. Teachers read a short piece of text aloud, slowly and usually more than once, and students try to write it down. A variation is the Dictoglos (Wajnrib, 1990). In this approach teachers read the text at a normal pace several times and students jot down key words and phrases. They pair up and together try to recreate the text. If desired, pairs can become a quartet and all four students try to make their text as close to the original as possible.

- **Cloze Listening**—Another way to scaffold the listening process is to prepare a semi-completed set of notes. These could take many formats: paragraph, outline, timeline, T-chart, Venn diagram, and more. The format could be deliberately matched to the text structure (e.g., timeline for chronological text). The content information is presented orally (by teacher read-aloud or by audio clip or CD-ROM), and the students add the missing information to the notes page. These note pages can be prepared in a differentiated manner, with more information on sheets distributed to the less proficient students.

- **I-Charts**—Inquiry Charts, or I-Charts (Hoffman, 1992), involve students in the planning process. Students generate questions about a given topic, and as a class, they decide which will be included in the inquiry process (approximately 3–5 questions). The questions are recorded on the chart and students add what they already know in response to each question. Then the teacher presents a set of materials (e.g., video clip, recorded speech or interview, or song), one at a time, related to the topic, which students listen to in turn and record what they learn on the chart. The chart can be used for summarizing orally or in writing. (See Cloud, et al., 2010 for a lesson example from a middle school beginning ESL class.)

The value of becoming a focused listener becomes clear in academic discussions. As we aim for rich discussions in class, we need the students to understand what their classmates and the teacher say so they can build on the ideas, agree or disagree, add more examples or counter-examples, and so on.

Scaffolds for Expressing Ideas

English learners need not only exposure to the type of language they will be asked to produce but also urged to produce language that becomes more sophisticated as they advance their English proficiency. Our job as teachers is to give them tools to articulate their ideas in the new language and recognize information presented orally. In brief, we want to help them know what to say and what to listen for.

One way to support student learning and practice with these verbal expressions is to post charts in the rooms with verbal scaffolds similar to those presented below. As with any scaffold, once students have acquired the phrases or language frames, the appropriate charts can be removed from wall, and new ones can be hung in their place as needed.

Recognize routine classroom language. Students start to notice routinized language early on in their learning curve. There are certain phrases and expressions that provoke an automatic response. A teacher may say "Open your textbooks to page 54," and a student needs very little time to process and act on the instruction, mostly hearing "Open . . . 54." It is useful to teach formulaic expressions, ranging from "How are you?" "Fine thanks, and you?" to "Please pass in your papers," "Exchange your homework with a partner," and "Turn and talk." Some of this routine classroom language will indicate an activity that students will do independently, in pairs, or in small groups. Listening for key words and phrases can reduce confusion and keep students engaged and on task. Formulaic expressions that are familiar can be used later as exemplars to point out grammatical notions like use of the imperative, subject-verb agreement, adverbs of time, and so on.

Teachers also use common expressions to indicate the importance of the information they are sharing with the students. Helping English learners hone in on phrases like the following gives them a way to focus their listening process:

- "This is very important."
- "Ok, here is something interesting."
- "Remember this for the test."
- "Underline this in your notebook."

- "Be sure to write this down."
- "Here's what you should study."
- "We will be adding to this tomorrow."

Teachers also use inflection, strategic pauses, and repetition to signal importance. Students must also be taught to pay attention to these speech features so that they learn to focus on important information and respond appropriately.

Teach classroom scripts. To build on the students' skills in listening for routine talk in the classroom, teachers can also introduce basic scripts and sentence starters that let them share their comments, ask questions, and participate in whole-class or small-group discussions. These scripts can be organized by language function to reflect the different types of verbal interactions that may take place. Teachers can model these scripts and let students practice the phrases with a partner. Figure 5.3 shows some sample scripts.

Explain signal words. In text and in speech we use signals to indicate a language function or a text structure. By explaining these cues to students and linking them to their purpose in the discourse, we essentially

> ## ACTIVITY
>
> Think about a day in your own classroom. Which scripts or sentence starters from Figure 5.3 do you tend to use? Do you use a script that isn't listed?

Figure 5.3 **Sample Routine Scripts and Sentence Starters for Classroom Talk**

Language Function	Script or Sentence Starter
Ask for Clarification	Please explain that again. What does ____ mean? I don't understand. Please repeat. I thought you said ____. Is that right? Could you say that another way?
Express an Opinion	I think that ____/I don't think that ____. I believe that ____/I don't believe that ____. My opinion/view is ____. In my opinion, ____. It seems to me that ____.
Take a Turn/Interrupt	May I say something? I have an idea. Excuse me. Let me jump in. Oh, that reminds me.
Build on Another's Idea	I have another idea. I'd like to add on. To piggyback on ____ idea, I would say that ____. I agree with ____ and would add ____. I had a different thought.
Report Back on Group Work	Our group decided that ____. We found that ____. Our answer/decision/response is ____. We have a few different ideas. We didn't finish yet, but so far we think ____.

give them some insider knowledge that allows them to process the information. If a student hears, "Both of these are . . ." she knows a comparison is being made. If another student hears, "If you combine two hydrogen molecules with one oxygen molecule, then . . ." he knows a cause/effect statement is being made.

Sarah Russell, a SIOP teacher in Washoe County, introduced us to her signal word charts in her classroom. She made ones for Compare and Contrast words, Cause and Effect words, Problem and Solution words, and more. Contrast words, for example, included the following: *however, but, on the other hand, different from, less than,* and *yet.* She taught her students what the words meant and encouraged them to look for them in text and use them in conversations. (See Russell's charts in Vogt & Echevarria, 2008, pp. 36–39.)

> ## Tips for Teaching Scripts, Signal Words, Sentence Starters, and Academic Language Frames
>
> 1. Do not introduce these scripts, sentence starters, and academic language frames to students all at once.
> 2. Teach one or two at a time. Give students time to practice using the expressions.
> 3. Post charts with the expressions on classroom walls. Add to the expressions over time, according to language function.
> 4. Consider taking down charts as students master the language frames.

Pull together sentence starters and signal words into academic language frames. Academic language frames offer an excellent way to support English learners' academic language development. These frames provide structure for using language to express higher-order thinking and to accomplish academic tasks. Students benefit when teachers present multiple language models of these academic frames to help them conceptualize the function in action. As students learn to use these language frames in classroom discussion, they begin to use them in their writing and recognize them in academic text.

Look at the examples in Figure 5.4 on the next page. Try to list additional ways to express these language functions. Think of another function that your students need to use in your class and include it in this table. (See Seidlitz, 2008 Vogt, Echevarria & Washam, 2015 and Zwiers, 2008 for further examples.) These academic language frames also can be charted like signal words, or combined with signal words, on classroom walls.

> ### ACTIVITY
> Think about three students in your class. How would each benefit from language frames? How might you adjust language frames for beginning and advanced English speakers?

Authentic Academic Language Models

We know that some students do not have strong academic English language models at home or in their neighborhoods. While we heartily recommend that students have rich discussions with their families on academic topics in their native language to help them develop knowledge, test hypotheses, practice argumentation, and so on, we also know we need to provide academic English language models for them in school. The metacognitive processes of analyzing and summarizing information, for example, will transfer to the new language, but articulating these analyses and summaries in academic English will need support.

One first step for teachers is to determine what oral language they would like students to produce. For example, if students are to explain their solution to a math problem involving sales tax, what would you expect a proficient speaker and excellent math student to say?

Figure 5.4   Academic Language Frames
Look at the language functions and sample sentence stems below. Add to the categories. In the final box, think of another language function and list possible stems.

Function	Stems	Function	Stems
Analyze	- The significance of ___ is . . . . - One reason ___ happened was . . . . - From the chart/timeline/ map, one can conclude . . . . - The graph indicates that . . . . - - -	**Compare/Contrast**	- A key similarity/difference is . . . . - ___ differs from/is similar to ___ in that . . . - ___however/whereas/ nevertheless . . . - In contrast, . . . - - -
Bias/Point of View	- ___ claims that . . . - In this text, ___ is arguing that . . . . - Based on this excerpt, a reader can conclude that ___ believed . . . . - ___disagrees with him because - -	**Define/Describe**	- ___ means . . . - ___ is an example of . . . - The diagram shows . . . - It has ___ but it doesn't have ___ - -
Cause/Effect	- ___ was caused by . . . - If ___ happens, then ___ - The result is ___ - Because of ___, ___ - -	**Sequence**	- First . . . second . . . finally . . . - In [month/year/date], . . . - In the past___ but currently . . . - ___ occurred while/ after/ before . . . - - -
Conclude/Evaluate	- For these reasons, we decided . . . - ___ is better than ___ because . . . - Based on the passage/ diagram/chart/map/timeline, we conclude that ___ - Of all the options, the least likely is . . . . - -	_____	- - - - -

Adapted from Seidlitz, J. (2008). *Navigating the ELPS: Using the new standards to improve instruction for English learners.* 2nd edition. San Antonio, TX: Canter Press.

What vocabulary terms and mathematical phrases would you like to hear? This reflection can help a teacher decide what language should be taught and modeled. Once this is determined, the teacher can seek out ways to demonstrate the language to the students. This can be accomplished in the following ways:

- Teacher think-aloud
- Audio recording of peers who can explain well
- Audio or video explanations online
- Teacher-recorded explanation

This math example is a fairly short utterance, but language models can be offered for more extended discourse, too. Technology affords us easy access to a seemingly endless stream of possible language models. Showcase video clips of speeches, debates, news broadcasts, plays, and similar types of more formal communication that fit the lesson goal. Devote some time to analyzing the communication style, discussing word choice, looking at gestures and non-verbal cues, and even examining the rhetoric with more advanced learners. Whatever form the model takes, it is important for teachers to match the selected clip with the objectives they have for the students' language production as well as their proficiency levels.

Multiple Opportunities for Practice

The old adage "Practice Makes Perfect" may be trite but it is true—with one caveat: correct practice makes perfect. Our students need correct models followed by frequent practice with listening and speaking skills in order to become proficient users of academic English. The practice regime starts with basics such as repetition of sounds and words taught. Songs, chants, raps, and poems can be utilized to focus on sounds and words plus rhymes, pronunciation, fluency, patterns of speech, intonation, and the like. We need to help students encode new words in oral forms, not just learn how to recognize them in print.

Software technology that allows students to speak and record their own utterances is valuable for English learners when used strategically. Being able to (1) hear a native speaker, (2) record their own speech, (3) compare their voice to the native speaker's, and (4) re-record gives students autonomy in their development and repeated practice opportunities. It is also motivating, satisfying, and nonthreatening. These computer programs, apps, and other technologies like podcasts align closely to language learning strategies we often recommend to students, namely rehearsing and self-monitoring.

Our goal in developing SIOP Model lessons is for students to have meaningful practice activities that link to language and content objectives. That means we would like the students to discuss the content topics but use targeted vocabulary, specific language frames, and/or grammatical structures to do so. There are many resources for teachers to consult for techniques that promote interaction in the classroom. Some are designed specifically for English learners (Echevarria & Graves, 2015; Herrell & Jordan, 2008; Seidlitz & Perryman, 2011, among others), and some resources for all students can be modified if needed for English learners (Buehl, 2009; Fisher, Brozo, Frey, & Ivey, 2007; Marzano, Pickering & Pollock, 2012, among others). Our SIOP books offer a large number of activities to meet the language and content objectives and provide numerous lesson plans showing how the techniques can be incorporated. The recently published *99 More Ideas and Activities for Teaching English Learners with the SIOP Model* (Vogt, Echevarria & Washam, 2015) is one place to start. (See Appendix B for a list of our SIOP books.)

Here is a sample of the types of activities we have in mind:

- **Targeted Questions**—The teacher creates questions based on the material covered in one or more lessons. The questions are written to either incorporate a question structure being studied (e.g., *Who?, Where?, What?, When?, How?, Why?*) or to elicit a language structure or function in the answer (e.g., "Tell how addition and multiplication are similar." "What are the differences between whole numbers and fractions?"). For a whole-class activity, the teacher may write the questions individually on cards or strips and place them in an empty container. Students choose one to answer and share with the class. For a small-group activity, the teacher may prepare fewer questions but repeat them, building sets for each student group. Students distribute the questions within the group and answer the questions.

- **Conga Line**—The teacher distributes index cards and asks each student to write something unique on his or her card that integrates the content being studied with a language target (e.g., "Describe your favorite character in a story using descriptive adjectives"; "Using the frame, 'I would like to be _____ because_____,' tell what element you would like to be and why"). Younger students may draw their responses to a prompt.

  The teacher then divides students into two equal groups and arranges the two groups in two lines but facing each other. Students should face a partner. Next, students in Group 1 share information from the index card with a partner from Group 2, and that partner comments. Group 2 students then share their information with the same partner from Group 1, who comments in turn. After a few minutes, teachers tell Group 2 students to take one step to the left so each person faces a new partner from Group 1. (The last person in Group 2's line moves to other end of that line.) Students repeat sharing the ideas on index cards. Teachers may repeat this process several times more.

  The value of this activity is that each time a student shares his or her information with a partner, s/he can adjust how it is said based on feedback received from earlier partners. Everyone in the class gets to speak multiple times to different partners in a fun, nonthreatening manner.

- **GIST**—This activity builds listening and summarizing skills. While students view a video or listen to a speech or lecture, they are to record 10 terms or phrases that capture the main ideas. They then individually or in pairs use the words and phrases to write a summary paragraph. They can also use the ideas to orally retell the information.

- **Radio Talk Show**—The teacher selects three or four of the more advanced students to be the radio show hosts. Other students draft questions they have on a topic. The questions to be asked may be assigned by Bloom's taxonomy (e.g., some students write an analysis question, some an evaluative one, some an application). The students take turns posing the questions to the radio hosts, who take turns responding. They might refer to function charts posted in the room to frame their answers. The talk show could be recorded and the speech analyzed at a later time.

- **Movie-making**—New technologies allow students to shoot video and make movies. They can write a script that incorporates language targets and enlist peers to play the roles. They can create a documentary-style video, conduct and film interviews, and record narration. They can also take photos and link them in a program like *Animoto*, adding narration and music.

Less Teacher Talk

Our final guideline may be the hardest for teachers to put into practice. As we mentioned earlier, teachers on average speak for 80% of the class period. We have got to change that percentage and vastly increase the amount of time students talk about the academic topics. In order to do so, teachers must practice verbal restraint; that is, they should rein in their instincts to share more and more information and to help the students out.

Let students finish their thoughts.   In our classroom-based research, we have seen the following scenario repeated many, many times. A teacher asks a question and a student begins to respond. The student may pause after only a few words, perhaps to collect his or her thoughts, find the right word, or clear a throat, yet the teacher jumps in and finishes the sentence. More often than not, this situation occurs when the student is at a lower proficiency level in English. When asked, some teachers say they did not realize they were doing this, while others say they did not want to put the student on the spot. Instead, we have to let students try to complete their responses and encourage them to speak out. One easy solution is for teachers to use Think-Pair-Share or Turn and Talk. Let students think about an answer, share it with a partner, thus rehearsing what they want to say, and then speak out. Allowing for more wait time (Feature 18 of the SIOP Model) is another way to foster opportunities for students to share their complete thoughts.

Play verbal ping-pong.   Teachers often think they are holding an interesting academic discussion with their whole class when they ask questions and select a number of different students to respond. What happens is that teachers ask a question, a student replies, usually with a one- or two-word response, and then the teacher follows up, usually with a paragraph's worth of discourse. Although 5 or 6 students might be called on (or sometimes fewer, with one or two doing most of the talking), the amount of time they speak is quite limited. To avoid this situation we advocate that teachers add three little phrases to their verbal interactions:

- "Tell me more."
- "What do you mean by that?"
- "Who can add on?"

These three phrases put the ball back in the student's court to provide more information. Or they allow another student to extend the discussion.

Ask higher-order questions.   We know that more than half of teacher questions are at the recall or basic comprehension level. If we want to generate rich discussion and have students produce elaborated speech, we have to ask better questions. Some teachers erroneously believe that because English learners do not know their new language well, they cannot respond to higher-order questions. This is not the case. They may take longer to compose an answer in their mind, they may speak more hesitantly or use some of their native language to explain their ideas, but if teachers practice the guidelines we have set forth in this chapter, they will have provided the students with schema and scaffolds to articulate their responses.

Teachers can plan higher-order questions with Bloom's taxonomy (Anderson & Krathwohl, 2001) and Webb's (1997) Depth of Knowledge framework. Higher-order questions can also be embedded within group projects. As students tap into their learning to conduct projects with others, they will also need to engage verbally in the actions required to complete the task. The result is students offering suggestions, negotiating roles or products, explaining or clarifying information, and more all in service of a project.

Application to Common Core Standards

As we noted earlier the Common Core State Standards mark a major shift in literacy and math education, as previously interpreted by highlighting listening and speaking as major elements of the English/language arts and constructing viable arguments and critiquing the reasoning of others in math. The need to teach students how to present their ideas orally, comprehend what is spoken, and collaborate with others through verbal interactions is clear. Helping students to shape their own ideas and reasoning through creative and critical thinking is desired, not the mere parroting of information. Through SIOP Model instructional practices teachers can make sure students are well positioned to reach these goals.

Let's look at the language demands of standards in ELA and mathematics:

ELA Anchor Standards 1 and 4 for Speaking and Listening, which is the same for all grades K–12, ask students to:

- Prepare for and participate effectively in a range of conversations and collaborations with diverse partners, building on others' ideas and expressing their own clearly and persuasively.
- Adapt speech to a variety of contexts and communicative tasks, demonstrating command of formal English when indicated or appropriate.

Math Practice Standard 3 across all grade levels involves, in part, that:

- Mathematically proficient students understand and use stated assumptions, definitions, and previously established results in constructing arguments.
- They make conjectures and build a logical progression of statements to explore the truth of their conjectures.

These complex standards require considerable knowledge and experience on the part of students to meet them. Students have to have learned how to use academic English orally for a variety of purposes and practiced it in numerous communicative ways with multiple partners. They have to organize their ideas, plan what they will say and react to what others say, and participate, even collaborate, in conversations or challenge another's reasoning. They have to know the difference between formal and informal academic English, and they need some sociocultural competence to determine when to use one or the other. Although Standard 4 focuses on speech, unless it is unidirectional (e.g., a student gives an oral presentation), the standard implies listening comprehension skills are necessary. For without listening to what another says, how might one know how to respond?

With SIOP Model instruction, students are prepared to meet these standards. One of the eight components of the SIOP Model is Interaction (see Appendix), and while the associated features clearly encourage "a range of conversations and collaborations with diverse partners" and "a variety of contexts and communicative tasks," they also demonstrate an understanding that students who are learning English as a new language need supports during the acquisition process. Teachers are asked to create lesson activities so students orally *interact with the teacher and with classmates to produce elaborated speech* (Feature 16), and the *grouping configurations* teachers use in class should meet language and content goals (Feature 17). In addition, teachers are reminded to provide students with *wait time* so students can plan their responses (Feature 18) and to allow for *clarification in the native language* if students do not know what is being said (Feature 19).

Additional SIOP features also support oral language development. The *language objectives* of the lesson (Features 2 and 24) can target speaking or listening skills and be delivered through *meaningful activities* (Feature 6). *Teacher speech* (Feature 10) and *higher-order questioning patterns* (Feature 15) can model or elicit specific oral language functions and structures. Lesson activities should help students *apply the language objective* (Feature 21) and *practice using all four language skills* (Feature 22). The *feedback* (Feature 29) provided in the lesson is also important in helping students improve their speech.

Remember the U.S. Government SIOP lesson on how legislation becomes a law in Chapter 4? Let's consider what might happen in subsequent days to follow up on this unit topic. Once students have learned the basic procedures for how a bill becomes a law—or doesn't if vetoed—the teacher might extend the learning process through a role-play of a Mock Congress.[1] This project taps the students' higher-order thinking skills and provides a strong opportunity to work on oral language skills in academic discussions.

This lesson lasts for about one week. The content objective is

> Students will conduct research on potential legislation.

The language objectives are

> Students will use persuasive speech to argue in favor of or against legislation.
> Students will draft a bill and write talking points to support its passing.

The first language objective addresses the CCSS ELA Anchor standards for listening and speaking discussed above. The second language objective addresses Standard 1 of the Anchor Standards for Writing in History/Social Studies, Science, and Technical Subjects: Write arguments to support claims in an analysis of substantive topics or texts using valid reasoning and relevant and sufficient evidence.

The teacher begins by spending 2–3 minutes with a personal connection—the role or purpose of school clubs—asking if anyone has been in a school club. Students share their experiences and describe club goals and activities. The teacher introduces the Mock Congress project and asks students to recall any committees in the House of Representatives they have already studied or have heard about. After the discussion, the teacher and students select five committees to focus on (e.g., Education, Armed Services, Foreign Affairs, Agriculture). The teacher assigns students heterogeneously across the five committees and randomly assigns political parties. Those in the majority party elect a Speaker of the House. One student from each committee is selected to be on the Rules Committee, too.

The teacher presents sample legislation from a committee that is not part of the lesson (e.g., Transportation). They discuss the wording of the bill. Within their committees, students discuss possible bills that could become law or an amendment to an existing law. Each student has time to research the potential legislation related to his or her committee's area of responsibility and then drafts a bill. The bill must be 2–5 sentences long and must explain the purpose of the law. It must be titled. Each bill is to be written on an index card, and the teacher offers possible language frames to use.

---

[1] Our thanks to Paul Giansanti and Alexander Meli, civics teachers at Brien McMahon High School in Norwalk, CT, for this concept. This is a modification of their lesson plan.

Before they start the next step, the teacher reviews the debate process for the committee discussions. As a class, the students identify ways to be persuasive, ways to agree, and ways to disagree politely. Bills are shuffled and selected randomly within each committee for consideration. The author tries to persuade his/her colleagues to vote for the bill. Colleagues ask questions. After a limited time for debate (e.g., 2–3 minutes per proposed bill), the committee votes for one of the following actions: (1) pass the bill as is to the Rules Committee, (2) amend the bill and then pass it to the Rules Committee, or (3) kill the bill.

Each committee then selects one bill among those "passed" (#1 or #2 above) to be sent on to the Rules Committee. They conduct additional research to find relevant facts, examples, and other persuasive information to share with the other representatives and add notes to the back side of the index card.

The Rules Committee members discuss and debate each bill received.[2] The discussion is led by the member whose committee proposed the bill. After two minutes of debate, if there is no consensus, members consult with colleagues on their original committees to find ways to influence the decision. When the full time is used up, the rules committee members vote one of three ways: (1) pass the bill on to the open House floor, (2) amend it and pass to the floor, or (3) kill it. Committee members then rank the bills in order of preference and the top two move to the floor of the House.

Before the students participate in the final debate and vote, the class watches a C-Span clip of debate on the House floor. While viewing, the students take notes on the formal phrases the legislators use (e.g., "I yield to the gentleman from Massachusetts."). After a discussion of what they viewed, the Speaker of the House then opens debate and sets rules for discussion. After five minutes of debate, each bill is voted on.

At the end of the final class, students pose one question they still have about the legislative process on an index card. The teacher arranges them in a circle and they pass the cards clockwise.[3] At teacher direction, they stop passing and the teacher randomly calls on some students to read aloud the card they are holding. If possible, students answer the question they have posed. Not all cards need to be read and answered. The teacher then finishes the Mock Congress with a review of the objectives and concepts learned.

Summary

English learners have not had the same exposure to oral English as native English speakers, so they require more extensive opportunities to apply the language. Many of the practices we advocate in this chapter will enable students to meet the speaking and listening standards defined in the Common Core and in other state standards. They will help them with communication goals in the science and math standards as well.

Keep the following points in mind as you plan your instruction.

- English learners need to develop listening and speaking skills using language functions and academic discourse patterns so they can participate in classroom discussions, whether they are explaining a geometric proof, presenting evidence for a scientific claim, or predicting the consequences of a fictional character's actions.

---

[2] Although this is not the procedure in Congress, the rest of the "legislators" watch the Rules Committee debate so they are available to respond to questions or provide additional arguments in favor of the bill.

[3] This activity, Pass the Note Card, is explained in the SIOP science book (Short, Vogt & Echevarria, 2011b, pp. 73–75).

- Teachers need to establish a safe, respectful, and positive classroom environment where students are comfortable taking risks with language.

- Teachers should offer students interesting topics to talk about, but must ensure they have enough background knowledge and vocabulary to do so.

- Students need explicit instruction on how to be active listeners; this can be accomplished by helping them focus on the key aspects of the spoken word. Teach them to be responsive listeners as well so they can respond to what they hear or build on classmates' ideas.

- Teachers must provide verbal scaffolds such as signal words and academic language frames to help students articulate their thoughts and contributions to classroom discussions.

- To help students distinguish between formal and informal English and to help them set a target for their own performance, teachers should share authentic models of spoken academic English with them.

- Teachers should ensure that models of correct speaking are provided so that students practice accurate forms and grammatical structures.

- As with vocabulary development, students need extensive practice with oral interactions in a variety of contexts. Practice should involve listening and speaking but be connected to reading and writing as well.

- Teachers should remember to let students do more of the talking in class, and to make sure they are given enough time to express their ideas fully.

Questions for Reflection

1. How does oral language development relate to the Common Core standards (or your own state standards)? How might the emphasis on speaking and listening skills impact your own teaching?

2. Read through the lesson plan presented on pp. 87–88. What scaffolds would you add for beginning English speakers? Rewrite the lesson and include specific supports for beginning speakers.

3. How would you summarize the conditions for effective oral language development for your colleagues?

4. A number of oral language techniques were described in this chapter. Find one that is new to you, or a modification of one you know, and describe how you might use it in a lesson.

Promoting Collaborative Academic Discussions

Fotolia

Chapter 4 focused on teaching academic vocabulary. Learning to recognize vocabulary words and determine what they mean is essentially a receptive skill. You see or hear a word you know, and its definition comes to mind. If it is a word you are less familiar with, you may reflect a moment before the meaning becomes clear, or consider other clues, such as nearby words, graphics, or gestures, to make sense of the term. Chapter 5 targeted teaching students how to express their ideas or questions orally. This is a productive skill in which you organize your thoughts and plan how you will say them aloud to convey meaning. You can use models, sentence starters, and language frames to develop skills in producing language.

This chapter pulls the receptive and productive skills together to help students generate the interaction needed in a classroom and beyond the school walls. The ability to communicate to a variety of audiences for diverse purposes is one key trait that makes us human. Learning how to listen and respond, craft an argument or counterclaim, and persuade someone else or change your mind when presented with new information are critical college and career ready skills, and, more importantly, life skills.

In Chapter 5, we presented guidelines to build students' academic oral language skills. This chapter takes those practices one step further to enable students to participate in rich academic discussions. These discussions can be led by teachers, but we will also aim for collaborative conversations in which the students can support one another as they co-construct knowledge and work toward creating a product or some other goal. The suggestions we offer in this chapter are not simply for classes with English learners; they apply to all classrooms where productive student talk can be enhanced.

Let's recap some of the points from Chapter 5 that teachers may want to keep in mind as they strive to design settings and scenarios in their lessons that motivate students to hold productive conversations.

1. Remember that a nonthreatening environment where individual ideas are welcomed and respected is essential so students are comfortable speaking out and are willing to take risks with language.

2. Topics that are interesting and promote student contemplation yield better academic talk.

3. In order to participate effectively in a conversation, a student needs to be a good listener. S/he must process information or utterances that are heard fairly quickly, retain the information that is said, compose a response, and then say it aloud.

4. Just giving the students more time to talk is not sufficient. The talk needs to be coached and scaffolded. Sentence frames and signal words can guide the students in articulating their thoughts, but these scaffolds must be removed as students master the process.

5. If we want students to talk like a historian or a scientist, we have to provide language models so they learn what it sounds like in terms of vocabulary usage, sentence structure, and rhetorical style.

Benefits of Collaborative Academic Discussions

We should be clear about the benefits to students when they engage in robust discussions on academic topics with their peers. Language learning is a social process, and through interactions with others, students have multiple opportunities to bolster their skills. The advantages of collaborative discussions include:

- **Exposure to more language.** We have already mentioned that effective language learners take risks with language as they practice new words, grammatical forms, and language functions, and as they receive feedback on their utterances. They use language to convey meaning as well as to clarify, negotiate, and co-construct meaning. They learn how to contextualize what they want to say and how to react to what others say. They make new vocabulary their own. Through these types of comprehension checks and dialogue, students learn more words, better phrasings, nuanced use of language, and, by the way, subject matter information.

Sample Language Functions That Can Be Practiced in Effective Collaborative Academic Discussions

- Provide examples and counterex-amples
- Analyze
- Synthesize
- Build on others' ideas
- Describe
- Elaborate
- Predict or hypothesize
- Connect
- Paraphrase
- Sequence
- Clarify
- Confirm
- Interrupt politely
- Restate or retell
- Sequence
- Summarize
- Report out

- Conclude
- Negotiate meaning
- Agree or disagree
- Support opinions
- Persuade
- Solve
- Consider/accept/reject suggestions
- Express multiple perspectives
- Listen attentively and remember
- Listen attentively and record information
- Distinguish fact from opinion
- Identify evidence
- Explain cause and effect
- Compare
- Justify
- Evaluate ideas and information
- Advise

- **Learning from peers with more advanced levels of proficiency.** When teachers and more proficient classmates expose English learners to language that is just beyond their independent speaking levels by interacting with them, they help the English learners advance to higher levels of language proficiency. This interaction also facilitates learning as these "more capable others" provide the right amount of information and support necessary to foster understanding (Vygotsky, 1978). Through social interaction, students are exposed to other people's points of view and discover how others respond in a variety of situations, which contributes to their language development and intellectual growth (Tharp & Gallimore, 1988; Vygotsky, 1978). The process of understanding others' viewpoints and explaining and defending one's own opinions and positions leads to valuable learning experiences as well as increased language proficiency for English learners.

- **More language practice time.** We mentioned in Chapter 5 that teachers need to talk less. If they do so, students will have the opportunity to talk more. In a whole-class discussion, students talk one at a time. But if students work with partners, 50% of the class gets to speak at the same time. In small groups of 3 to 5 students, 20%–33% may be speaking. Researchers have found that teachers typically provide few opportunities for English learners to speak in content classrooms (Arreaga-Mayer & Perdomo-Rivera, 1996; Verplaetse, 2001). We have to change the dynamic because the students won't learn academic English well without practice.

- **Culturally responsive classrooms.** Giving students a role in sharing information in a discussion helps promote a culturally responsive classroom. If we achieve our goal of creating a classroom where students are known and respected, and where they feel understood by the teacher, students will be more comfortable sharing their perspectives and experiences on issues and topics that arise in the lessons. By building on students' life experiences, teachers can more easily elicit their worldviews and promote more cross-cultural understanding (Nieto & Bode, 2011). But to do so, the discussion prompts have to be open-ended; they should not be the known-answer questions that teachers commonly ask. Small-group settings can be advantageous for students to build rapport with one another.

Making Collaborative Academic Discussions Work

Many teachers may hesitate to develop lesson plans that set aside a considerable time for student group discussions. Although teachers recognize the value in the endeavor, it may be challenging to share responsibility, release control of the classroom, and hold back from sharing all the important information they know about the topic at hand. They may also worry that students won't pull their weight or that the information students co-construct will not be correct or of sufficient depth. Some fear that the least proficient students will remain silent and unengaged. But in fact, researchers have found that learners are more engaged academically when they work in small groups or with partners than when they are in whole-class settings or working on individual assignments (Brooks & Thurston, 2010). By providing students with opportunities to interact with one another, to discuss and work on authentic problems, and to test possible solutions, teachers give students tools that often lead to higher achievement (Mergendoller, Maxwell, & Bellisimo, 2006; Wiggins & McTighe, 2008). Further, the use of collaborative discussions does not mean the teacher relinquishes all responsibility for checking on student understanding of a topic or for enriching it.

The guidelines in Figure 6.1 will help prepare you and the students for rich academic discussions.

Figure 6.1 Guidelines for Collaborative Academic Discussions

1. Teach students rules for discussion.
2. Align the type of discussion to lesson objectives.
3. Ask good questions to prompt academic discussions.
4. Teach students how to ask questions.
5. Link oral discourse with reading and writing.
6. Hold students accountable for their talk.

Rules for Discussion

Participating in an academic discussion does not come naturally to anyone. Even children who join in with the family dinner table conversation have to learn to take turns, listen to others, not interrupt, be respectful, and more. In some cultures, children are not expected to participate in discussions, so they come to school with even less experience in doing so. In our classrooms we want to teach our students rules and procedures for the kinds of productive discussions that are expected in American schools. Some teachers like to model appropriate behavior with a fishbowl technique. They pre-select students who know how to participate well and give them a task. It may be a small-group discussion with the teacher or just with other students. As the group discussion ensues, the teacher may pause at times to call attention to something one student has just said or asked.

The following are some common rules teachers in our research have reported setting in their classes.

- **Take turns**—Teachers stress the importance of ensuring all students have the chance to speak during academic discussions. It is helpful to involve the students in establishing some standards for turn-taking and for generating ideas as to why taking turns is important.

  When some teachers use a whole-class setting, they pull student name sticks from a jar to prevent calling on the same one or two students all the time. Some of these teachers will put the pulled name sticks back in the jar after several minutes so all the students stay engaged. Teachers may call on a student who is unable to answer but then return to that student, perhaps to have him or her repeat what another person responded (this happens more often with students at low proficiency levels) or to add on to another student's response.

  To help students take turns when they are in small groups, teachers offer other techniques. One is to assign roles to the students—one role being the Stage Manager whose job is to ask for opinions or comments from all group mates. Another is to give one or two tokens to the students. When they speak, they put a token on the table or desk. They can't speak again until all students have spoken and all tokens have been placed down.

  As students learn to understand the importance of balanced turns, teachers may move to encouraging self-selected turn-taking. Discussions are enhanced when students aren't required to wait to be called on; they initiate their turn to speak.

- **Stay on topic**—Having students stay faithful to a topic is a critical aspect of effective academic discussions. Providing a purpose for the discussion, a product that is the result, and a fixed time for the interchange are three tips teachers have shared with us. It is important for teachers to circulate and listen to the discussions to ensure the students stick to the topic.

- **Express ideas clearly**—This rule is one that students (and even adults) work on all their lives: conveying our ideas unambiguously to a conversational partner. Add in cross-cultural communication norms and it can be a challenge for students in our classrooms. Our suggested signal words and language frames in Chapter 5 provide a scaffold for helping students express themselves clearly. With guidance they can learn to align the purpose of their comments to appropriate language functions and then build a repertoire of academic language frames to use.

- **Listen actively**—We addressed this partially in Chapter 5 but want to repeat its importance here. When students are actively engaged in academic discussions, they are listening closely to their classmates' comments and they are weighing how these comments fit with their thoughts. Ideally, they adjust their comments to what has already been said. They may add to a comment or refute it. What we want to avoid is students just waiting for an opening in the conversation or their turn to talk without following what already has been shared.

- **Build on others' comments**—This rule follows active listening closely. Students need to realize that if a member of the discussion group has made a comment highly similar to what they planned to say, they need to adjust. This is better than declining to comment at all. They can agree ("I agree with . . .") and they can agree and add more ("I agree with . . . and would add . . . ."). Similarly, if they disagree or have another example, they can provide some transition ("I disagree. My idea is . . . ." "I have another example . . . .") to show how what they plan to say is connected to what has been said.

- **Be respectful**—It is important for students to learn that being respectful of one another is paramount in academic discussions. If they disagree, they must do so politely. If they are surprised by a comment, they may say so, but politely. If a peer mispronounces a word or uses incorrect grammar, they should try to make sense of the meaning, not call negative attention to the mistake.

- **Initiate comments**—Students should not be passive during an academic discussion. Everyone should contribute ideas or ask questions. To make this happen successfully teachers may need to prepare the students—making sure they have background knowledge of the topic, know vocabulary words related to it, have practiced different language frames, and most importantly have some time to gather their thoughts before engaging with others.

- **Allow for wait time**—Just as we work with teachers to provide more wait time for their students to respond, we want to teach students to wait for their classmates as well. Students must learn not to hem and haw. However, students who struggle to share an idea benefit from supports, such as having a peer who can interpret the idea from a native language into English or being given the opportunity to sketch or act out a response. In one classroom where the teacher established a caring atmosphere, when a student struggled to complete a sentence, she asked, "Can anyone help your friend?" and others volunteered to express what the student tried to say. Sometimes a student will just not have anything to contribute and so giving each student a "pass" token may be one way to keep the discussion on track.

- **Generate multiple exchanges**—Ideally a teacher will have demonstrated some productive academic discussions to the class, through a technique like fishbowl discussed above or through video clips. These models will show that a good discussion involves multiple collaborative comments among the participants. Through back and forth interaction that includes many of the points raised already (e.g., listening actively, building on others' ideas, disagreeing politely, initiating comments, and staying on topic), students can deepen their knowledge of a topic, test and accept or reject hypotheses, and even let their imaginations soar as they suggest solutions to problems.

- **Play your assigned role**—If the teacher has allocated roles to group members (e.g., recorder, reporter, illustrator, monitor), students should play their role as best they can. In some cases, a teacher may need to review the roles and responsibilities. However, it is important that having a role like illustrator does not mean a student is not expected to contribute to the discussion.

- **Be prepared**—For some academic discussions, students will have to prepare information in advance. They may need to read some text, interview some people, conduct some Internet research, and learn new vocabulary and language frames. When they get together with their group mates, they need to be ready to actively participate, whether they will be debating, planning a TV talk show, or presenting a report on a science experiment.

Formats of Academic Discussions Aligned to Lesson Objectives

Once students learn how to participate in a productive discussion and monitor their own behavior, they can be prepared for a variety of formats including one-to-one, small-group, and teacher-led discussions. In the SIOP Model we remind teachers to align their grouping configurations to lesson objectives because the activities should serve as opportunities for students to make progress in their learning targets, particularly those associated with language. Moreover, all students, including English learners, benefit from instruction that has variety—arrangements such as whole class, partners, triads, small groups of 4 to 6, and individual tasks. Groups may be homogeneous or heterogeneous by gender, language proficiency level, language background, reading ability, and so on. However, teachers should make deliberate decisions about grouping students, not indiscriminate ones.

- **Teacher-led discussions**—These are common in all classrooms but have some disadvantages, which we mentioned earlier. Teachers may talk too much, they may call on only a small number of students, and they may elaborate and extend student ideas rather than ask students to do so. Nonetheless, there is a role for teacher-led discussions in the classroom, which may be for the whole class or for a small group of students, as during guided reading. Whole-class groupings are beneficial for introducing new information and concepts, for modeling procedures, and for conducting previews and reviews. Teacher-led small groups can allow for direct instruction on particular skills that a student group needs to learn. Further, a small-group setting is typically more comfortable for eliciting student participation, and it allows the teacher to utilize the language opportunity strategies we have mentioned throughout this book, such as prompting for more elaborated responses, redirecting a comment, and asking students to explain their answers. Whether in a whole or a small group, the teacher uses his or her expertise to skillfully guide active participation by all students.

ACTIVITY

Do Whole-Class Discussions Foster Student Language Practice?

Whole-class discussions led by teachers may generate a lot of talk, but most of it is by the teacher. Yet the teacher doesn't need the language practice. Try this activity. Video record a lesson in which a whole-class discussion is scheduled to take place. This may be one of your classes or that of a colleague. Afterward, watch and count the number of times the teacher speaks and the number of times each individual student speaks. Who speaks more frequently—the teacher or the students? Do all students have a chance to say something? Do only a few students speak most of the time? Next, measure how long each person speaks. This can be done with a stopwatch or just by counting the number of complete sentences spoken. What do you discover?

- **Partner conversations**—Paired talk, or one-to-one talk, can be very effective in classrooms with English learners. If teachers pair students with more proficient speakers, they scaffold the participation process. More proficient speakers have an opportunity to practice using academic English, exercise higher-order thinking, and negotiate meaning with peers while less proficient students have the support needed for completing academic tasks and exposure to models of more advanced English expression. In our research, middle school English learners reported that they benefitted from working with partners because of the repetition, collaboration, and English practice it provided.

Teachers employ various means for pairing students. Sometimes it is as simple as "Turn and Talk" to a neighbor. Sometimes it is a pairing by native language. Sometimes it is more complicated, as in the CREATE history study where classes were almost evenly divided into English speakers and English learners. Those teachers rank-ordered the English-speaking students by their reading ability levels and the English learners by their English proficiency levels. Then the highest ranked in each group paired up, the second highest ranked were matched, and so on (Reutebuch, 2010). Having students close to similar levels enabled peer-assisted learning to take place more smoothly. Teachers could spend more time with the less proficient students and allow those who were ranked higher to work more independently.

Paired discussions can be highly structured, as is the case when specific roles are assigned to Partner A and Partner B, such as interviewer and respondent. In this example, one student asks questions about a topic or text and the other responds. The interviewer may prompt or restate as necessary in order to elicit information for meeting the lesson's objectives. Partners may reverse roles so that both students have the opportunity to assume each role.

- **Small-group discussions and projects**—Small-group discussions can promote the development of multiple perspectives on academic topics. However, these interactions must be carefully planned and carried out to yield gains in oral language (Saunders & Goldenberg, 2010; Seidlitz & Perryman, 2011). In their review of research on oral language development, Saunders & O'Brien (2006) found that effective classrooms do not just give students more time to talk; they coach the learners in how to talk.

To help encourage collaboration, teachers often give each student in these groups a role. Depending on the lesson's objectives, roles might include a leader who facilitates the discussion, a recorder who writes down important points generated in the discussion, a checker who verifies statements by consulting the text or other source, and a reporter who serves as a spokesperson for the group's conclusions. By assigning roles, students know what is expected of them during the discussion, and it increases participation and engagement since the discussion has a specific purpose for each participant.

For accountability, teachers might give points for participation based on teacher observation. Students may also be asked to rate their group mates' participation using a rubric. These evaluations would be in addition to points given for successful completion of a task or for individual contributions.

Teacher Questions to Stimulate Academic Discussions

Teachers lead by example. It is important to practice and model good questioning techniques for students. When teachers pose questions, they should be sufficiently clear so students can answer, but also worded in a way that stimulates thinking and discussion. As we pointed out in Chapter 5, if you want students to have an interesting conversation, you need to begin with an interesting question.

Teach students question words and other prompts like function and process words.   Whether students hear a question that would prompt a discussion orally or see it in writing, they need to recognize it as a question or a directive to respond to. Certainly beginning-level students need to learn the 6 Ws—*who, what, when, where, why, and how*—and will do so with explicit instruction. But there are numerous times when the question words do not come at the beginning of the question, so the key word is embedded. We see this in math exercises, for example. Consider: *Given that x is greater than 6, what whole number could x be if it is also less than 8?* Students have to be taught to interpret *what whole number* as the question to focus on even though it comes halfway through the statement.

We often find that imperatives that represent a language function or a process indicate questions to answer in academic discourse. Consider this example: *Compare the achievements of the Babylonians with the achievements of the Egyptians. Compare* tells students what they need to do, namely make a comparison, but none of the typical W-question words are present.

We know that both examples—embedded question words and functional word-related prompts—appear in standardized tests. By teaching students to recognize these types of questions and prompts, we help prepare them for some of the accountability measures they face.

> ### ACTIVITY
>
> Look over the past few tests or quizzes you have given to the class. Also look at some released items from the state standards-based tests. Identify the test question words and function words that tell students what to do. Notice if they are embedded or if they appear at the beginning of the question. Make a list of common question words and function words to share with your class.

Pose questions that drive higher-level thinking.   Good questions are often linked to themes. They may be called *essential questions* or *guiding questions*. They do not have easy answers. They are offered specifically to challenge students to draw on information they already know and information they have gained over the course of a unit, so cumulative knowledge is necessary to answer them.

Questions can be grammatically simple but call for critical and/or creative thinking among the students. For example, the following two question prompts ask for the same information. One, however, is simplified to promote student understanding. Can you tell which is which?

> 1. We have studied three French explorers. Think about their achievements. Which is the greatest achievement? Why?
>
> 2. As you know we've been studying three French explorers of the New World. All of them had some achievements but I'd like you to consider which achievement you think is the greatest among them and provide a rationale.

The first prompt is more straightforward. The ideas are divided into separate sentences and the question words are transparent. If students are in heterogeneous groups by proficiency level, all have a chance to understand Question 1 and participate in a discussion about it. Question 2 might be introduced at another time to present to students the more sophisticated phrasing of a question one might find on a test, but then the language objective for that lesson might focus on interpreting test language rather than on promoting oral discussion.

Don't ask trite questions.   Another point to keep in mind is to avoid banal questions. By that we mean questions that don't generate thinking, such as "Do you understand?", "Okay?", and "Who wants to answer?" Students can sit back in their chairs, nod their heads, or wait for others to answer. Teachers ask these types of questions many times every day. You might catch yourself doing it because it is so common. If you want to know whether students understood a portion of the lesson's material, have them turn to a partner and share something they learned; or they can jot it down on paper, stand and walk around, and at a signal find a partner to share with. After that you can ask who had similar comments and who had different ones. These more engaging activities take little more time than asking trite questions and waiting for answers.

Student Questioning

To sustain academic discussions and make them as productive as possible, we want to teach students how to ask appropriate academic questions when they are working with their peers. The following suggestions might be posted on a chart in the classroom as a reminder. Additional ideas might be solicited by the students themselves:

- **Know the purpose of your question.** Students need to think about the reason they are posing a question. They can ask themselves: Am I asking a question to:
  - clarify something someone just said?
  - confirm what I thought someone said?
  - generate an example from the text?
  - have someone make an observation?
  - generate a justification for a claim?
  - define a term?
  - elicit a connection to something else studied or read?
  - tap someone's background knowledge or experience?
  - draw a conclusion?
  - generate a summary?
  - make a prediction?
  - have someone elaborate?

- **Stay on topic** As with the discussion comments in general, the questions posed have to stick to the topic or task. If the discussion revolves around a piece of text, the questions should relate to the text or its topic. The questions may inquire about an author's point of view or choice of words, make an inference or a prediction, examine use of imagery, or more. Questions may also relate to the topic, but must be focused and tie specifically to what is discussed in the text. It is often tempting to bring up ancillary questions that don't relate directly to the text, but these can sidetrack the students. Students must learn to formulate questions that enhance the discussion but nonetheless stay on topic.

- **Pose questions that advance the discussion.** In a nutshell, the goal of academic discussions is learning. For that reason we do not want students to get in the habit of asking the same or similar questions over and over again in their groups, creating a circular or redundant conversation. However, they might use routine questions to keep the discussion moving, such as:
  - "Can anyone give us another example?"
  - "Does anyone have more to add?"

- o "Does anyone disagree?"
- o "What haven't we thought of yet?"

- **Adjust questions to peers' proficiency levels.** This may seem like a difficult guideline for students to meet; however, because students are often aware of what each other is capable of academically, they can be taught to adjust the discussion based on individuals' proficiency levels. It may be more difficult for students who are not native English speakers or advanced-level English learners to do so, but it is possible to convey to students that a grammatically complex question or a question with several unknown vocabulary words or idioms can stall a discussion.

Teachers must remember that just exhorting students to ask good questions and follow these suggestions will not be sufficient. All students need some structured practice in learning to ask questions that target the task, advance the discussion, and match their peers' level of understanding. Teacher modeling and the fishbowl technique are two ways to accomplish this, with partner and small group follow-up practice. Some teachers invite students to pose as the teacher and ask questions to the class as a way to practice these question types as well. Certain research-based techniques, such as Reciprocal Teaching (Palinscar & Brown, 1984), can also be taught. See Figure 6.2 below.

Oral Discourse Linked to Reading and Writing

We find the curricula at some university English language institutes for international students learning academic English puzzling: there are ESL reading classes, ESL writing classes, and ESL discussion classes. We wonder: Why separate the language domains this way? Why not address all four language domains with the same topics and themes? That is the more natural approach, isn't it? We read something in the newspaper and talk about it with a colleague at work. We write an email and read the response. We read a review of a movie, go to see it (which involves listening, too), and talk about our reactions afterward. We discuss an assigned project with a partner and then do some research before starting it.

As we have mentioned elsewhere, second-language acquisition research shows the value of developing the four language domains together (August & Shanahan, 2006;

Figure 6.2 Reciprocal Teaching Technique (Palinscar & Brown, 1984)
This research-validated technique helps students cooperatively develop comprehension from text through group conversation. It can be applied to fiction and non-fiction reading passages. Students work in groups of four, with each assigned a different role.

1. Assign roles: Summarizer, Questioner, Clarifier, and Predictor.

2. Introduce or review the process that occurs in this order: **summarizing**, **questioning**, **clarifying**, and **predicting**. Provide sentence frames (e.g., For summarizing: "The gist of the passage is . . . ." For clarifier: "Do you mean . . .?") and let students practice.

3. Be sure the students are clear about the type of conversation they should have with their peers during each step of the process.

4. Assign a short text to the group and identify places in the text where students should stop reading and have a reciprocal teaching conversation.

5. Student roles may be rotated.

After students are familiar with this routine, let them determine where in a reading they should have reciprocal conversations.

Geva & Yaghoub Zedeh, 2006; Saunders & O'Brien, 2006; Tarone & Bigelow, 2005). It is a synergetic process. Knowledge acquired through one domain (e.g., listening) can be applied in another (e.g., writing). We advocate, therefore, that reading and writing be linked with speaking and listening in structured ways that build on skills students have and advance those skills in complementary ways.

Scaffold the reading process.   If we want students to have a rich discussion about a text, we may have to scaffold the reading process. When English learners are unable to read a text by themselves, the mechanics of reading dominate the lesson. For students who are focused almost completely on decoding the text, the essence of a collaborative discussion is greatly reduced. They may be able to recall facts, but analysis and inferencing are considerably more difficult. This is an important point to keep in mind with the use of complex text in Common Core classrooms. The use of grade-level text that is above students' independent reading level requires some scaffolding to help them gain meaning. These scaffolds may involve the following:

- **Teacher-led read-alouds**—Teachers read text aloud, sometimes with pre-reading activities and always with some during-reading discussions. Teachers may be used to reading fiction aloud, but it is also beneficial for them to read non-fiction and textbooks aloud and share their thought processes with the class (Layne, 2015).

  - **Pre-reading**—Teachers explain abstract concepts through explicit building background activities so that students are able to participate in the subsequent discussion. Using text about Martin Luther King, Jr., for instance, a teacher presents the concept of *prejudice* and elicits students' individual reactions and experiences regarding fair and equal (or unfair and unequal) treatment.

  - **During reading**—Several times when reading text aloud, teachers pause to tie the topic to background schema already developed, explain new vocabulary that may not have been pre-taught, or model a comprehension check or connection ("I wonder why . . ." ; "This reminds me of . . ."). Teachers should decide in advance how they will chunk the text, where they will pause, and what specific questions they will ask in order to capitalize on students' own knowledge, experience, and/or comprehension of the text.

- **Partner reading**—Student pairs take turns reading to one another. One variation is Read Aloud, Think Aloud. One partner reads a paragraph and then summarizes it. The other agrees, disagrees, or adds to the summary. Then the second partner repeats the process with the next paragraph.

- **Small-group reading**—Often used in guided reading classrooms, teachers organize students into ability groups and work with them as they read a common text. Teachers can pinpoint decoding, comprehension, or analysis issues the students have. Even though it is more frequently found in elementary schools, this also can be used effectively at the secondary level. The teacher creates a small-group reading station in the room that he or she supports and has planned other activities not requiring close teacher guidance for those students outside the small group.

- **Audio-supported reading**—Audio books can support students' oral language and literacy development, if students follow along with the written text. The recordings provide students with models for pronunciation, oral fluency, and pragmatic information such as how to chunk parts of a sentence (e.g., by noun phrase or prepositional phrase) when reading aloud. For students whose spoken English is better than their reading skills, hearing the words read aloud can aid in comprehension.

- **Digital Jump-start**s (Rance-Roney, 2010)—Teachers use digital storytelling technology (e.g., *Photo Story, iMovie, Movie Maker*) and the power of images and sound to build background and vocabulary as a pre-reading tool. The scripts, image selection, and captions can be customized for the English learners' language proficiency levels and can incorporate or reinforce specific language targets (e.g., sentence structures, vocabulary reinforcement) or cultural targets (e.g., understanding the women's suffrage movement before reading a biography of Susan B. Anthony). It is an alternative to a traditional jump-start, which is small group–and classroom-based and does not offer repeated exposures to the new information and vocabulary. Digital jump-starts can be set on classroom computers or tablets for students to view and review. They can be downloaded onto DVDs students can take home or uploaded to free websites that host video clips and digital media (e.g., YouTube).

These types of scaffolds allow students to understand the text so they can participate fully in discussions. Post-reading, no matter what kind of scaffold was used, teachers will want to summarize the key ideas and check students' basic comprehension of the information. They may review key vocabulary as well as some of the background building links covered earlier before students are asked to discuss the reading more deeply.

Co-construct knowledge of the text with collaborative discussions. Plan collaborative learning tasks about the readings with pairs and small groups to promote the use of oral language—to persuade, defend claims, analyze characters' actions, and more. In our research, an 8th grade student who decoded at the 2nd grade level made important contributions to the discussion of a grade-level novel when the story was read aloud and she followed along.

One research-based approach that embodies this guideline is Instructional Conversations or ICs (Dalton, 2007; Echevarria, 1995; Goldenberg, 1992–1993; Tharp & Gallimore, 1988). ICs emphasize meaningful discussions and promote active student participation. Through ICs, students have the opportunity to learn targeted concepts and language as they talk about text. As the name implies, these conversations promote oral language but are also instructional. The teacher functions as a facilitator to encourage students' contributions about the topic and allows students self-selected turns so that they take ownership of the conversations. The teacher also chunks the text into sections to provide maximum opportunity for discussion and relates students' background experiences to a text-based discussion. Students are asked to support their comments with evidence from the text, which is consistent with practices supported by the Common Core and other state standards.

Strengthen the writing process with collaborative discussions. The image of a solitary novelist tapping away on a keyboard is perhaps more a figment of the imagination now than a reality. Many novelists and other writers share ideas and drafts of their material in writer's groups and at writing workshops. Open any book and you will find the author acknowledging colleagues who have read versions of the text and given feedback. Likewise, we want our students to be comfortable using their oral language skills to improve their writing. The following are some techniques teachers in our research studies have employed in class:

- **Oral Brainstorm**—Students discuss their ideas for individual or joint texts that they will be writing. When working in groups, one student might keep track of the ideas, jotting them down, and another might play the role of cynic to guide the group in winnowing down the list.

- **Read-Write-Pair-Square**—After reading a selection, students respond to a prompt in writing. They pair up and share their written responses, perhaps looking for similarities or unique perspectives. The pairs square up, that is, form a quartet, and share again. Some teachers have the first pairs choose one of the two responses to share in the square if time is limited.

- **Peer editing**—Student partners edit one another's written work. Generally, teachers explicitly model how this type of editing should occur and provide a rubric or a list of key traits or skills to focus on, such as use of synonyms, use of punctuation, development of the main idea, and so on.

- **Author's Chair**—A student presents a finished piece of work to a small group or the whole class. The class listens and provides feedback. Usually this is done after the writing has been edited.

Student Accountability

To ensure effective academic conversations, teachers need to hold students accountable for their participation in all formats of discussions as well as their contributions to products that result from the discussions.

Make expectations clear. Teachers should share their expectations for participation with the students. These outcomes may vary by the type of discussion or the product. By practicing structured conversation routines in advance, teachers can set the goals directly, modeling appropriate comments and feedback. For products, teachers might show a sample of completed work so students know what is expected. Further, for projects and other more long-form products, teachers often use rubrics to guide students and assess their work. We recommend these rubrics include items related to the academic discussion process. Some teachers have students self-report their level of participation and also rate the participation of others in their groups.

Teach students to use evidence as a basis for their comments during discussion. Increasing students' use of evidence in text to discern details, explain character interactions, determine author viewpoints, and compare information are among the many targets in standards for college and career-readiness. Teachers should explain to students that their comments in a collaborative discussion need to be grounded in fact or reality. Even if a student is offering an opinion, he or she should support it with some evidence. Citing text evidence or referring to ideas that were explored orally provides a basis for a productive discussion.

The following language frames can help students refer to text evidence.

1. "I see on page _____ that it says _____. So, I agree with your point."

2. "The author's purpose was _____ (e.g., to show kindness to those in need). It says right here, _____, which demonstrates the author's purpose."

3. "The type of text structure is _____ (e.g., sequence). I know it is _____ (e.g., a sequence of events) because the text uses terms such as _____ (e.g., *in the year 2003, next,* and *finally*)."

Give students responsibility for judging participation. Ownership is given to the learners, which encourages them to work together more productively and participate more fully in discussions. The teacher models how a rubric is used to distribute points for participation. Some categories might include *active participation*, *thoughtful responses*, *building on others' comments*, and *citing text evidence*. During discussions, the teacher circulates and makes comments that reinforce how students will recognize whether a student's participation warrants points. Often when students are put in charge of their own learning, it makes them better learners. However, the process requires proper preparation and modeling to ensure success.

ACTIVITY

Think about your own class. How do you stimulate discussion? Which ideas can you incorporate into your teaching? Complete the chart below.

How I stimulate discussion now	New ideas I can use in future lessons

---

Application to Common Core Standards

In Chapter 5 we discussed which language skills students needed to accomplish ELA Anchor Standards 1 and 4 for Speaking and Listening and how the SIOP Model features support students developing oral interaction skills. These skills are needed in collaborative academic discussions as well. The guidelines that we have explained in this chapter play a vital role in productive conversations, such as being accountable for your comments and following rules for discussion, including taking turns, listening attentively, and building on others' comments.

As we think about further application of the Common Core State Standards in academic discussions, we perceive how other standards can be addressed too. A major goal of the Common Core ELA standards implementation is richer discussions in class about texts that students are reading. So, for example, Anchor Reading Standards 1–3, focused on Key Ideas and Details, could be targeted through a small-group discussion format after students have read a text in common. Research has shown that these types of discussion yield benefits in terms of reasoning and reading comprehension skills (Applebee, Langer, Nystrand, & Gamoran, 2003). These standards for grades K–12 are below:

- Read closely to determine what the text says explicitly and to make logical inferences from it; cite specific textual evidence when writing or speaking to support conclusions drawn from the text.

- Determine central ideas or themes of a text and analyze their development; summarize the key supporting details and ideas.

- Analyze how and why individuals, events, and ideas develop and interact over the course of a text.

Merge them with Standard 1 of Speaking and Listening

- Prepare for and participate effectively in a range of conversations and collaborations with diverse partners, building on others' ideas and expressing their own clearly and persuasively).

and it is clear how oral discourse can support reading comprehension. In our work as part of the CREATE research, where the SIOP Model was the professional framework for a schoolwide intervention and the Word Generation curriculum (which incorporates discussion and debate) was implemented in ELA classrooms, we found that students developed academic language skills in vocabulary knowledge and argumentation, both orally and in writing (Snow & White, 2012).

So, a number of SIOP features will help teachers provide instruction that supports CCSS-driven student learning. First, let's review the Interaction features again: frequent opportunities *for interaction and discussion with the teacher and with classmates to produce elaborated speech* (Feature 16); *grouping configurations* that support language and content objectives (Feature 17); *wait time* for students (Feature 18); and occasional *clarification in the native language* (Feature 19). Next consider other features that bolster these reading and oral language goals, such as planning *meaningful activities that integrate lesson concepts with language practice* opportunities for reading, writing, listening, and/or speaking (Feature 6); offering *clear explanations of the academic task* (Feature 11), so students will know what they are to accomplish in the collaborative discussion and how; and providing ample *opportunities for students to learn and use learning strategies*, such as those used for reading comprehension (e.g., predicting, summarizing, visualizing, self-monitoring, and evaluating) (Feature 13). Practice and application features come into play, too: Activities to *apply content and language knowledge* in the classroom (Feature 21) and activities that *integrate all language skills* (i.e., reading, writing, listening, and speaking) (Feature 22).

Let's see what a collaborative discussion might be like. Recall that it is more than a series of questions and answers; instead, it is a conversation that engages all students. Notice how the teacher prompts and guides the discussion, but participation is student dominated. Also note how the skills emphasized in the standards mentioned above are practiced throughout the following discussion:

Teacher:	Our theme has been the American Dream. We've read three related articles and watched a video about it. So, now what do you think of the American Dream?
Jordan:	I think that it's all about opportunity. The opportunity is there if you want it.
Ana:	But what do you want?
Nathan:	What do you mean?
Ana:	What you want is what the American Dream is to you.
Robert:	Are you saying, like, what was in the article said that it has changed? Like it says here, *For many, the American Dream has shifted from a pursuit of freedom and equality to a pursuit of money.*
Ana:	Yeah, it's what you want and most people want to be rich.
Alexis:	Well, everyone has his own life. I don't think about being rich because I just want to eat everyday and get a good job. Depends on your life, I guess.
Jordan:	Well, at least you have the opportunity in this country to do it.

Teacher:	Do you agree that there is plenty of opportunity for all in the U.S.? What did Mr. Jacobs say in the video?
Alexis:	I don't agree with what he said about opportunity.
Teacher:	What Jordan said or Mr. Jacobs?
Alexis:	Jordan. He acts like if you want it you can have it.
Robert:	Yeah, it's not so easy.
Ana:	Well, Mr. Jacobs said that opportunity is disproportionate in society. I agree because some people have rich parents and some have to work really hard for everything.
Jordan:	I thought you said everyone wants to be rich.
Ana:	I said that most people want to be rich but I guess for some it is what you want. So, the American Dream could be just a house and car or a job or whatever.
Nathan:	Like the other article about Oscar, my parents came to this country hardly with anything and worked hard. Now sometimes people treat me like we're rich but I know how hard they worked. You can't judge people.
Teacher:	Ok, so do you all agree that the shift in the American Dream that we read about is real?
All:	(indicate affirmative)
Teacher:	Ok, then, let's turn our attention back to the issue of opportunity. Let's look again at the article "Opportunity in America" and discuss the survey results regarding the American Dream.

[Discussion continues after re-reading the selection.]

Notice the self-selected turn-taking that is similar to adult conversations. The teacher facilitated the discussion and guided its direction; the students stayed on topic and used readings and video as a basis for their comments. This brief glimpse of a collaborative discussion shows how active participation by all students is possible and provides them with opportunities to express themselves orally.

Summary

Being able to hold a productive and collaborative academic discussion is a measure of success for students' English language development. In order to have rich, robust discussions, students have to put together information learned with information known and use English to convey their ideas, make comments on others' ideas, and react to the give and take of a synchronous interaction.

Keep the following points in mind as you plan your instruction.

- Share your expectations with students and teach them the rules for effective academic discussions. For each rule, provide models and time to practice.

- Alter the formats for discussion in your lessons. This variety will spice up the classroom and also allow students to practice appropriate participation in whole-class, partner, and small-group settings. Decide the type of format according to your lesson objectives.

- Remember that if we want students to have a discussion, we have to give them a good reason to converse. So teachers and group mates need to ask good questions, both to prompt the discussion and to keep it advancing.

- Students receive many benefits from collaborative academic discussions. They have more time and opportunity to practice using the language they are learning and may be willing to take more risks in partner and small-group formats. They can learn from their peers—new vocabulary and expressions as well as new perspectives and ways of thinking about problems and issues.

- We also have to hold students accountable for their participation.

Questions for Reflection

1. How do collaborative academic discussions differ from traditional class discussions? In what way are they similar? What are the benefits of collaborative academic discussions?

2. How might English-speaking peers contribute to richer academic discussions with English learners?

3. Which of the rules for effective academic discussions are most relevant for the students in your own class? How will you teach the rules to your students?

4. Some teachers are reluctant to use collaborative groups regularly in their lessons. How would you persuade a colleague to start?

5. Review the section on teacher questions to stimulate academic discussions. Write at least five questions that will drive higher-order thinking for your students.

7

Advancing Academic Language Proficiency

Fotolia

In this chapter you will

Content Objectives:

- Identify three commonly used interactive language skills.
- Contrast syntax and semantics as they relate to a grammatically correct sentence.

Language Objectives:

- Write language objectives of increasing complexity for use with English learners.
- Discuss how to implement specific ways of advancing your students' language proficiency.

1. John sees a cat.

2. John sees an orange cat.

3. John, who is wearing denim shorts, sees an orange cat.

4. John, who is wearing denim shorts and a red cape because he wants to jump out of his bedroom window and be Superman, looks down as he is falling and sees a cat that is the color of marmalade on the ground where he is about to crash.

Look at the four sentences above. Think about the student writers in your class. Which sentence most resembles the type of writing they produce? If you have beginning-level English learners, they may have only mastered the basic subject-verb-object pattern of sentence #1. Some may be able to insert a modifier like *orange* to add a bit of detail to their idea and might know to change *a* to *an*. We often see students, both English learners and native-English speakers, max out at sentences like that in #3. It is a big linguistic and cognitive leap to sentence #4, which still has the basic "John sees a cat" but adds on relative clauses, compound predicates, subordinate clauses, prepositional phrases, and more. Although such sentences are not called for in most academic situations, wouldn't we want students to be able to produce sentences like #4 from time to time?

As educators, we have worked with many students whose academic English is *good enough*—good enough to pass content area classes, good enough to communicate with native speakers, but not at a fully proficient level. Moreover, they are not thriving in school; they are only getting by. Our goal for these English learners, however, is full proficiency, so how can we help them reach it?

As we have discussed in prior chapters, academic English is syntactically and lexically complex (Snow & Uccelli, 2009). Some students plateau in their language development because they no longer receive services; they have completed all courses available but are unable to pass the proficiency exam. Others pass that exam but are not reclassified as fully proficient because they cannot pass other required tests such as a standardized English language arts assessment (Saunders & Marcelletti, 2013). Some switched programs continually (e.g., bilingual for two years, then ESL for two years, then bilingual again) and never developed literacy in any language (Menken & Kleyn, 2009). Many of these learners are known as *long-term English learners* (Freeman & Freeman, 2002).

We have an increasing number of long-term English learners in our schools—students who have been in language support programs or who have not tested out of English learner status despite 6 or more years of instruction (Olson, 2010). One feature that educators have noticed is that many of these students have a "Swiss cheese" knowledge of the English language system. In other words, they have gaps in their knowledge base. They may know how to express ideas using the future or past tenses, but they do not know how to use the past conditional or the future perfect. They may struggle to understand nominalizations or embedded clauses in text passages. They may write informational paragraphs with simple sentences and organized ideas, but they can't write persuasive essays.

It is important that language and content teachers work together to increase these learners' academic language skills. The language teacher covers the full scope and sequence of an ESL curriculum for the students at their proficiency level while highlighting the appropriate skills for the academic content courses the learners are studying. The content teacher reinforces many but not necessarily all of those ESL curriculum elements (e.g., vocabulary, sentence structures, reading and writing skills) and also shows how they are applied in the particular subject area discipline.

How Do We Advance Our Students' Academic English Skills?

The purpose of this chapter is to offer some guidance for assessing gaps in our students' knowledge and then addressing them, based on our experiences in SIOP classrooms over the past two decades and interviews with SIOP educators. We are focusing on those students who have seemingly plateaued in their language development at a high intermediate or advanced level overall and are still considered English learners or struggling readers or writers by district guidelines. We begin with a framework of academic language development so we can consider the potential scope of the problem.

ACTIVITY

If you work in a state that uses the WIDA (World-Class Instructional Design and Assessment) Standards for ESL, look at the Can Do statements for guidance as to what is appropriate and can be expected at different proficiency levels (www.wida.us). Organized by language domains and core subject areas, this resource can help teachers plan instruction and activities that meet and advance students' abilities in reading, writing, listening, and speaking. For classes with students at different proficiency levels across language domains (e.g., less proficient in writing than in other areas), these statements can inform the teacher of what to expect and how to move them forward.

A Framework for Academic Language

The framework in Figure 7.1 is a visual representation of academic language elements and skills. It may be helpful for assessing student progress toward becoming proficient in academic language and subsequently for planning language objectives and lesson activities. As students reach intermediate and advanced stages of language acquisition, there may be some areas where they lag behind and others where they excel. Using this matrix as a checklist, teachers can record which skills and elements of language a student has mastered. Patterns may emerge, such as a lack of mastery of inferencing and interpreting reading skills across a class that can help teachers generate appropriate language objectives for future lessons. Teachers also may use the results for individualizing instruction, particularly for those learners who have stopped advancing in their language development.

The matrix offers one of many ways to conceptualize academic language. The left column refers to language skills. We regularly talk about the receptive skills—listening and reading (and viewing fits as well)—and productive skills—speaking and writing—when we discuss language acquisition. We know that we develop these skills in tandem and that by strengthening one, we strengthen the others. These four language domains (i.e., reading, writing, listening, and speaking) have traditionally been assessed in isolation on standardized language exams.

This chart also adds an interactive category that focuses on combinations of skills because practical language usage frequently involves more than one skill. For example, both listening and speaking are needed for conversation. Besides interpreting what we hear, we have to be responsive to it in order to continue a discussion. We don't form our response out of the blue; we connect it to our conversation partner's comment or question. In other words, one person makes a statement and the other listens, reflects, and then responds. The first person does the same in turn until some closure is reached. Another interactive combination common in classrooms is reading and writing. Students read a selection in a text and are asked to write a response of some type, perhaps to answer questions about the content, give an opinion, or compare it to something else read.

These skills are applicable in social and academic contexts. We have conversations with friends, family members, and even strangers every day. We listen to music, television broadcasts, and public address systems in stores. We read signs, symbols, text messages, and stories. We share our opinions aloud. We write notes, cards, and emails. We respond in writing to emails and texts we receive. However, the cognitive challenge of exercising these skills is generally higher in school. The amount of information we have to call on to accomplish school tasks related to these skills is greater than in social settings and is usually more specialized.

The second column reflects subskills, showing some of the complexity of developing and using academic language skills in school. Not all possible skills have been listed, but the selection reflects an increase in sophistication as one moves down the rows. Consider the following in terms of the *receptive skills*:

- **Alphabet**—Learning the names, sounds, and visual representations of the individual letters in the Roman alphabet is the first step for our English learners who have a native language with a different writing system or a variation of the English system.

- **Phonemic awareness**—Recognition of the *phonemes*, the sounds that are the smallest units of words and word parts in English, is needed to begin reading and listening comprehension of words and sentences. That is, separating *bat* into 3 distinct sounds—/b/, /ae/, and /t/—requires phonemic awareness. After students develop alphabetic knowledge and print awareness, they should begin working on sound (phoneme)–symbol (letter) relationships, which is typically referred to as *phonics*. A solid understanding of these relationships is necessary before learning to decode words through sound blending.

- **Sight words**—These are commonly used words that account for up to 70% of the words used in beginning print materials. Young children are encouraged to memorize these words as a whole by sight, so that they automatically recognize them in print without having to use decoding skills. Many of these words, which are compiled on sight word lists, have unusual spelling patterns and cannot be sounded out using basic phonics knowledge (e.g., *eight, who*). Reading words by sight facilitates reading fluency.

- **Decoding**—Decoding is the ability to apply knowledge of letter–sound relationships, including knowledge of letter patterns, to correctly pronounce written words and construct meaning. Understanding letter–sound relationships gives children the ability to recognize familiar words quickly and to figure out words they haven't seen before. As we encounter words that are unfamiliar in academic text, we can decode word parts, such as roots and affixes, as we strive to determine meaning.

- **Fluency**—Good readers are fluent readers. Reading fluency is the ability to read text with appropriate speed and accuracy. It is a unique and fundamental component of skilled, proficient reading because of its close link to comprehension and motivation (Hasbrouck & Tindal, 2006). Students who read with fluency are more likely to read for pleasure and enjoyment, which increases overall reading proficiency.

- **Basic comprehension**—Construction of meaning moves beyond words and phrases into sentences, and then longer discourse. We seek to comprehend what we read and hear. At a basic level, we know the gist of the information, some key points, and some details.

- **Inference and interpretation**—As we develop proficiency in academic language, we progress beyond basic comprehension to various levels of inference and interpretation. At this point we are proficient readers and listeners—pulling knowledge together, and connecting, analyzing, and evaluating it as well.

The sophisticated use of language follows a similar pattern among the *productive skills,* but there are some additional cognitive processes related to producing language. Besides receptively recognizing sounds and words and making meaning, we have to produce language—at a basic level pronouncing and writing words accurately—so others may make meaning of our expressed thoughts.

Figure 7.1 A Framework for Academic Language

Language Skills	Vocabulary					Language Functions	Grammar/ Sentence Structure/ Mechanics	Text Structures	Prosody & Paralinguistics
	Basic/High Frequency/ Survival	Subject-Specific/ Technical	General Academic	Roots & Affixes & Morphemes	Synonyms & Antonyms	Symbols & Semiotics			
Receptive: Read & Listen	Alphabet								
	Phonemic awareness								
	Sight words								
	Decoding								
	Fluency								
	Basic comprehension								
	Inference/ Interpretation								
Productive: Write & Speak	Alphabet								
	Basic encoding: Write/Say words, simple sentences								
	Fluency								
	Planning & Organization								
	Complex encoding: Elaborate/cohere/ develop								
	Editing & Monitoring								
Interactive: Receptive + Productive	Above + Responsiveness								

Elements of Academic Language

© 2014, D. Short

112

- **Alphabet**—Some of our students need to learn how to form and say the letters of the alphabet, especially for letters that represent English sounds that don't exist in their home language. Handwriting practice might be needed for print and/or script.

- **Basic encoding**—Generally, we learn to write and say words and labels first, and then move on to phrases and writing simple sentences or speaking them aloud. We have to learn English syntax in order to form accurate sentences.

- **Fluency**—Proficient speakers and writers can produce language smoothly. While time may be taken to compose a thought that will be uttered or spoken, once planned, it is expressed without much hesitation. To promote writing fluency, some teachers regularly include daily writing practice.

- **Planning & Organization**—We plan before we produce. For school assignments, we think in advance about what we want to say or write. We organize our thoughts, and our skill in doing so improves over time with appropriate supports and more exposure to complex language use. This is an area of language development that some long-term English learners struggle with; they benefit from explicit instruction and practice in planning and organization of their thoughts, ideas, and expression.

- **Complex encoding**—As we gain proficiency, we can develop our thoughts and expression further, elaborating, adding detail, making our ideas coherent and cohesive. Text or oral expression that is cohesive has elements that are linked together (e.g., *It is a sunny day. We are going to the park. We should have a nice time.*). A text or utterance is coherent if it makes sense, as does the previous example. However, it may be cohesive (ideas linked together) but incoherent (meaningless) as in: *It is a nice day at the park. The park is far away. We stayed close by. We like the park.* In this case, the ideas are linked but make no sense. We learn to express coherent and cohesive ideas over time with instruction and practice.

- **Editing & Monitoring**—Effective speakers monitor what they say, sometimes correcting the pronunciation of a word the moment after it is uttered when they realize the error, sometimes rephrasing a statement to enhance clarity. Effective writers similarly edit what they write. They reread, looking for errors in spelling, grammar, and mechanics. They also determine whether the writing makes sense and successfully conveys the thought that was intended. In other words, proficient users of a language regularly edit and monitor what is said or written to clarify, correct, or improve it.

The *interactional skills* require all of the above skills and practices to be successfully accomplished along with responsiveness. We have to process input, comprehend it, plan a response, and encode the response. Or, we might produce oral or written text, judge how it is received, and then respond or adjust what was produced. We are continually decoding and encoding in an iterative fashion in order to co-construct meaning with another person or a piece of text.

When we think about using academic language skills in school, we recognize that students use all the skills in this second column. But it is the skills that require higher cognitive functioning (comprehension, inference, interpretation, development, and elaboration) that most clearly distinguish academic language from everyday language.

The top rows of the framework represent the elements of language applied in academic settings.

- **Vocabulary**—This element is further divided into subcategories:
  - Basic words, which include high-frequency words, survival terms, routine social expressions (e.g., "How are you?"), and the like
  - General academic or cross-curricular words mentioned earlier
  - Subject-specific and technical terms that are used less frequently but are critical to understanding content topics
  - Roots and affixes
  - Synonyms and antonyms
  - Idioms and phrasal verbs
  - Symbols and other semiotic systems

  All of these subcategories of vocabulary convey meaning and provide a necessary knowledge base for using academic language. Cognates can fit across several of these subcategories, but recognizing a cognate is a language learning strategy we would want students to learn and utilize. Other subcategories could be added, too, such as polysemous words that might confuse students who know one meaning, but not another meaning that is relevant to the lesson topic (e.g., *legend* on a map vs. *legend* as a tale).

- **Language functions**—These functions describe how we use language for a specific purpose—to describe, compare, or predict, for example. Words and expressions that we would choose when we want to persuade someone are typically different from those we would use to report on an observation or retell a story. Students may be able to understand and generate language related to some functions but not all. Pay attention: Can a student compare but not summarize? Evaluate but not analyze? Which language functions need to be explicitly taught? Understanding key words and language frames that signal these functions can help students comprehend oral and written text and can improve their production of language as well.

- **Grammar/Structures/Mechanics**—The structure of the discourse is another element that students need to master. This category includes grammar usage (e.g., conditional verb tenses, articles with count vs. non-count nouns), language structures (e.g., comparative adjectives), sentence structures (e.g., interrogative, sentences with relative clauses), and mechanics (e.g., punctuation and capitalization). In particular, this element focuses on syntax, or the general rules for arranging words to create phrases, clauses, and sentences that have meaning. Note that you can follow the rules for creating a sentence but still not make sense. Think of Lewis Carroll's "The Jabberwocky," which follows English syntax but is hard to understand due to the plethora of nonsense words.

ACTIVITY

In 1957, Noam Chomsky wrote "Colorless green ideas sleep furiously" to demonstrate that one could use proper English grammar to write a sentence but still create nonsense. Think of a similar example. How would you explain the parts of speech to your students? Why is it syntactically correct but semantically wrong?

- **Text structure**—The purpose of spoken or written discourse can dictate the text structure. Is the text comparing two events, explaining events in the order they occurred, or describing one event? Common text structures include description, comparison/contrast, cause/effect, sequence, problem-solution, and question-answer. Teaching students about text structure can help them make meaning of unfamiliar passages.

- **Prosody and paralinguistics**—The final column refers to non-verbal aspects of language, which are not tied to word choices but are linked to tone, intonation, stress, and gestures that accompany speech. The non-verbal expressions that accompany speech—intentional or not—may be as important as the words spoken. A spoken message always has a verbal and a non-verbal component. Non-verbal communication, particularly gestures, can be culturally determined and differ across countries, thus making it an aspect of communication that must be learned by some English learners.

ACTIVITY

Think about an English learner you know at an intermediate or advanced level of proficiency. Use the matrix in Figure 7.1 and record that student's skills. Put a plus sign in boxes to show what has been mastered, a check to show what the student is making progress on, and a minus sign for what has become stuck or is not well learned.

Now that we have discussed the various elements of academic language represented in Figure 7.1, we can turn our attention to analyzing students' current performance as well as designing and implementing interventions to advance their language development. This process is critically important. Figure 7.2 lists some steps that teachers can consider as they purposefully guide the academic language development of their students.

Figure 7.2 Guidelines for Advancing Language Proficiency

1. Diagnose gaps in academic English knowledge and performance.
2. Plan interventions and monitor regularly.
3. Ramp up language objectives.
4. Deepen vocabulary knowledge.
5. Extend oral language practice opportunities.
6. Apply oral language practice and vocabulary knowledge to academic writing.

Diagnose Gaps in Academic English Knowledge and Performance and Monitor Regularly

We need to find out why students are not making progress in academic English; there are several diagnostic tools we can use to do so.

- Examine test results carefully. In many states, results on the English language proficiency test report subskills that students have mastered or not. Look at these carefully to determine where the English learners are currently in their language development. It would be helpful to have 2–3 years' worth of data for comparison. One particular area, such as writing, might be the reason students do not pass the exam, and once this is determined, teachers can prepare a targeted intervention.

- Consult the students' other teachers. In a quick email, you can ask the other teachers of the students who have plateaued in their language development what they have noticed language-wise in class. Where do these students struggle? If they are experienced teachers, even if they are not ESL certified, they may be able to compare the students in question to others they have taught who have been able to transition out of the ESL program.

- Use the matrix in Figure 7.1 and record information you have about each student. Think about the skills in conjunction with the elements of academic language. For example, can students recognize content words but not write them, or are they able to use some words when they write but fail to use synonyms to make their text more interesting? Can they write basic sentences, like the first and second examples at the beginning of this chapter, but not more complex ones? Reflect on the language functions they are able to produce. Can students retell but not summarize? Evaluate but not synthesize? When they read, do they pay attention to the text structure to tap schema that might aid their comprehension? In some cases you may ask students to read aloud and think aloud with you so you can gain insight into how they process text cognitively, what connections they make, and what they stumble over.

Plan Interventions

Doing "more of the same" is unlikely to make much of a difference for students who are no longer making progress. Having students retake the highest level ESL course, for instance, is not our recommendation. Instead, consider the following actions:

- Once a review of the students' language performance has been conducted, plan an appropriate intervention. In most cases, all students will not exhibit the same issues. In other words, some may need help with certain writing traits (e.g., word choice, organization), while others may need to improve their higher-level reading comprehension skills. As a result, students should be grouped with others in need of similar skill building, and the interventions should be individualized as much as possible.

- Utilize technology to plan lessons for these students. Many activities for reading, listening, and writing can be supported through computer programs and apps. Our students may need some direct instruction (e.g., how to combine sentences, how to modulate one's voice for a persuasive speech), but due to their language abilities they can also work independently part of the time. Technology can also be used for oral language practice and the interactive skills that proficient users of English engage in. They can communicate orally and in writing with students in other classes or people around the world. They can collaborate on projects as well.

- Offer students choices. Many students, especially long-term English learners, are disengaged from learning for a variety of reasons. Sometimes students aren't motivated because they don't see the relevance of lessons and assignments. Personalizing learning by tapping into students' interests and capabilities can spark enthusiasm. Rather than having lessons remediate the areas students aren't competent in, use their areas of strength as springboards for skill development. Try having students set goals for themselves. Allow them to take ownership of their learning. Provide them with choices in terms of reading materials, topics to explore, projects to complete, and ways to express understanding, (e.g., a multimedia project, a written report, or a creative product). Students are more likely to re-engage in learning when we capitalize on their interests and abilities.

- Be sure to monitor the students' language development regularly with assessment rubrics, reading records, and other measures of growth. Many computer programs now gather data on users' progress and can report the results back to teachers. It is not advisable to wait until the end of a semester to ascertain whether the intervention helped the students as expected.

Ramp Up Language Objectives

When many teachers begin implementing the SIOP Model, they start by writing language objectives focused on vocabulary. Some add objectives that call for reading skills or speaking skills, but they may not include much variety or much focus on subskills or specific language targets. In order to advance the language proficiency of the learners, we need to increase the level of difficulty and the language required to meet the language objective successfully. For instance, we have viewed lessons with an objective like this:

> Students will discuss the causes of the Great Depression in small groups.

This is a good start for a new SIOP teacher; she is promoting oral language practice by providing the opportunity for group discussion, but depending on the needs of the class, the objective could be more focused as

> Students will discuss the causes of the Great Depression using cause/effect terms such as *because*, *as a result*, *caused*, and *effect*.

or

> Students will discuss and evaluate the causes of the Great Depression in order to determine the two most important ones.

The use of "in small groups" in the first objective above is part of the grouping structure and is valuable in a SIOP lesson, but the objective does not indicate a language target to be used in that discussion. The second objective gives clear instructions to students as to which terms to use during the discussion and the teacher can observe whether those terms are spoken or not. The third pushes the discussion beyond a list of reasons to an evaluation, requiring higher-order thinking and articulation of the judgment. This objective gives less guidance on how to articulate the ideas and might be better suited for more advanced students who know how to express the conclusion their group reached.

Another consideration is that in some cases it is worthwhile looking outside the topic for sources of language objectives. When content teachers incorporate language objectives into their lessons, they start with the topic being studied and determine an appropriate objective aligned to that topic. However, we recognize that not all of the language needs that the advanced learners have will be met in this fashion. That is why it is critically important for the

ESL or ELD teacher to work with a scope and sequence of language goals for the students. We want to ensure that all aspects of knowing a second language are covered. This can be accomplished in the ESL or ELD programs where students have had several years of instruction but should also be reinforced where possible in content classes. As the chart in Figure 7.1 shows, full proficiency in academic English involves knowing and applying discrete grammar points, discourse markers and text features, reading comprehension skills, vocabulary, and more. The results of the diagnostic review can help set language objectives for the learners.

Deepen Vocabulary Knowledge

Suppose in your diagnosis you notice that your students have good range of vocabulary but not a deep one. In their writing, for example, they repeat words frequently rather than use synonyms. In Chapter 4, we emphasized the importance of academic vocabulary development and offered a number of techniques to teach words (as we do in many of the other SIOP books). In this chapter we want to present some techniques that deepen vocabulary knowledge in order to boost students' reading comprehension of academic texts, their writing abilities, and their speaking performance.

- **Shades of Meaning**—This activity helps students focus on word choice, particularly the nuances among synonyms. Teachers may introduce this activity by showing students a paint chip card that shows a progression of shades of one color from lighter to darker. These shades all use the same base color but vary by intensity. The same point is made about synonyms. *Happy, content, delighted,* and *gleeful* are all adjectives expressing happiness, but they are not at the same level. Students can be taught to arrange the words by intensity, so this list might be *content-happy-gleeful-delighted.* When they understand the subtle distinctions among the words, students can improve their reading comprehension and their writing. This activity works for verbs, nouns, adjectives, and adverbs.

  There are several ways to introduce this activity to students.

  1. You might provide four words and have student pairs or groups decide how to organize them (e.g., *jog, dash, run, walk*).

  2. You might give students three words and ask them to find a fourth (e.g., *pretty—?—beautiful—exquisite*).

  3. You might ask them to think of a word they use too often and generate alternates (e.g., *cool*).

ACTIVITY

1. What word might you insert between *guess* and *hypothesize*?
2. Can you think of 3 or 4 words to build from *rarely*?
3. If *starvation* is in the middle, what words might come before and after it?
4. Think of a word and create your own shades of meaning with 3–4 additional words.

- **Transforming words**—Students can expand their vocabulary knowledge when they recognize how words can be transformed into other parts of speech. In Chapter 1 we described nominalizations, when verbs turn into nouns, a regular occurrence in many

Figure 7.3 **Transforming Words Chart**

	-tion	-able	-ful
consider	**consideration**	**considerable**	
respect		**respectable**	**respectful**

science texts (e.g., *condense/condensation*; *rotate/rotation*). Adding different suffixes to a root or to base words can transform words too.[1] Consider that *attract,* a verb, can become *attractive,* an adjective, and that *vocal,* an adjective, can become *vocalize,* a verb, or *vocalization,* a noun, or *vocally,* an adverb.

One technique recommended by Benjamin and Crow (2013) is to create a matrix with suffixes heading the columns and roots and base words at the start of the rows. Students would then determine if words can be made for the intersecting cell, as in Figure 7.3.

- **Idioms**—Native speakers of a language use idioms without much thought or awareness that their meaning may not be universally understood. Idioms like "It's raining cats and dogs" or "I'm on pins and needles" are not literal expressions, but are used to convey an idea or emotion. Exposure to the language over time and interaction with native English speakers increases students' opportunities to learn idioms, but they can also be taught explicitly in class. An idiom's meaning needs to be learned as a unit, not analyzed word by word, because the meaning does not derive from the combination of meanings of the individual words. Although idioms are used more frequently in social interactions than in academic discourse, they are often used by teachers and peers as part of classroom discussions and are found in stories and literary texts.

- **Collocations**—Collocations are words or terms that occur together more frequently than chance would predict and that are used as fixed expressions. Examples include *take advantage of, manual labor,* and *discuss with [someone].* Native speakers use them fairly naturally, and while they might not know why one expression, such as *bird house,* is accurate and a similar one, such as *bird home,* is not, they recognize almost instinctively expressions that are not correct. Collocations are best taught as units. Unlike idioms, their meaning can be determined by examining the individual words in combination.

  Collocations are formed in primarily six ways by combining parts of speech:

  1. adjective + noun—*fast food* (but not *slow food*)
  2. noun + noun—*ice cube* (but not *snow cube*)
  3. verb + noun—*take a test* (but not *take homework*)
  4. adverb + adjective—*happily married* (but not *sadly married*)
  5. adverb + verb—*strongly disagree* (but not *powerfully disagree*)
  6. verbs + prepositional phrase—*advise against doing* (but not *advise against to do*)

---

[1] Adding prefixes does not transform the word into another part of speech, but is also a valuable process for students to practice to deepen their word knowledge.

Phrasal verbs are common examples of the sixth type of collocation above. Determining the correct preposition that should be associated with a given verb can be a source of confusion to English learners.

- **Academic Fixed Expressions**—In addition to collocations and idioms, there are some academic fixed expressions that students can learn as semantic units and use in speech and writing (see Figure 7.4). A quick check of student expository writing will help teachers determine whether explicit instruction is needed in learning and using these types of expressions. Having students find examples of these expressions in their textbooks is one way to analyze their purpose and usage. (For more information see Alves, Berman & Gonzales, 2013; Liu, 2012; and Wray, 2000.)

Figure 7.4 Examples of Academic Fixed Expressions

according to	in general	from the perspective of	in contrast
as a result	a large number of	in addition (to)	on the one hand
as an example of	for example/ instance	based on	on the other hand

Extend Oral Language Practice Opportunities

In the SIOP Model we include a component focused on oral language interaction because we know that English learners benefit from speaking and listening practice to support their literacy development and we realize they typically speak up less in regular classrooms than native speakers (Verplaetse, 2001). In Feature 17 we remind teachers to move away from one- or two-word responses to questions and instead to elicit elaborated speech from their students. For our students who need a push to develop full proficiency, we recommend a focus on extended speech.

- **Academic language frames organized by proficiency level**—One step a teacher can take is to utilize a reference that provides examples for increasing the sophistication of student speech related to language functions. The academic language frames can be organized by proficiency level to guide teachers as they prompt students to voice their ideas. Because the frames are graduated in language complexity, students of all proficiencies can interact fully in class.

  Consider the following ways to articulate an argument and/or cite text evidence:

  1. I believe that _____.

  2. In my opinion, _____.

  3. I read in the text that _____.

  4. One historian argues _____, but another claims _____.

  In this list, the frames become increasingly academic, and the final example could reasonably be found in a professional journal. Our point here is to remind teachers to keep pushing their students to higher levels of expression, not to settle for students using sentences like #2 and #3.

  These academic language frames have merit in both oral and written discourse. If students begin to use these frames orally, they will then use them in writing and recognize them in text they read.

- **Multiple genres of oral language**—Our students need practice with multiple genres of oral language just as they do with multiple genres of text. It is possible that some English learners use English in a limited manner outside of school. They may not speak it very much in their neighborhoods, and while they may watch television, go to the movies, and listen to popular songs in English, these are receptive practices and not productive ones. Therefore teachers can set up activities and projects in which students engage in extended speech. This will allow them to create coherence among their orally expressed ideas and use a variety of paralinguistic measures such as adjusting pitch and intonation, voicing emotion, and using facial expressions to convey meaning. Examples of these multiple genres include:
  - Broadcasting the news for television
  - Narrating a documentary with the sound off
  - Presenting a formal speech
  - Participating in a formal debate
  - Teaching the class how to do something
  - Giving a toast
  - Reviewing a movie for radio
  - Interviewing a "celebrity" or "historical figure" for a magazine
  - Reciting a poem

Apply Oral Language and Vocabulary Knowledge to Academic Writing

Writing is one area in which most everyone can improve. Native English speakers and English learners, published authors and kindergartners alike can become better writers. When our English learners plateau in the area of writing, it is not because they aren't capable of writing a more detailed sentence or a longer paragraph; it is often because their ideas haven't been fully developed or their written expression has not advanced to a more sophisticated level. Frequently students receive instruction that encourages them to "get their ideas out" or "find their voice," which is a reasonable way to initiate the writing process but is not sufficient means to make someone an excellent writer. Our students often need to focus on form and sentence combining, and they may need work on organization and word choice as well.

- **Prewriting**—One of the most important prewriting activities for English learners is being given the opportunity to discuss their ideas. After they have read a text, have students write an outline of the information they plan to write about (or create a storyboard with younger students). Then, allow students to explain the outline of their ideas to a partner or teacher. The partner can ask clarifying questions, make suggestions, ask where the information is found in the text, and so forth. Talking about the topic before writing about it jump-starts the flow of language and identifies areas that need more work prior to putting pencil to paper (or fingers to keyboard).

- **Editing**—One way to help students improve their writing is to teach them how to peer edit.[2] If your school uses a systematic writing program that teaches traits of writing,

---

[2] Of course, it is important to teach students to self-edit as well, but it is sometimes easier for second language learners to edit another student's writing because the text is new to them and errors, overused terms, vague expressions, and other issues are not of their own making.

each trait can be addressed in turn (Graham et al., 2012). For example, to improve word choice, students can draw on their deepening vocabulary knowledge to replace overused terms. Reading aloud a piece of text will also help English learners make use of their emerging oral language skills as they seek to determine what sounds right and what doesn't.

- **Modeling predictable patterns**—Teachers and students can examine complex sentences in the texts that they are reading for predictable patterns. They might observe the occurrence of academic language frames and academic fixed expressions, the structure of the sentence, and/or the punctuation. Teachers can model common complex sentences such as those with *because*, *if*, and *although* clauses, using everyday topics at first and moving on to academic ones. Teachers can also ask students to do some discovery learning, and by looking at examples, try to generate their own rules.[3] Once the rules have been identified and clarified by the teacher as necessary, the students can then generate their own sentences.

  Embedded clauses can also be taught through modeling using everyday topics. The teacher can model using embedded clauses to describe the students: "Harry, who always wears a cap, will go first." The teacher can encourage students to use embedded clauses to talk or write about people, places, and events that are familiar to them. Then the students can use embedded clauses to discuss the content. "Linear equations, which require inverse operation, are easy to solve." "Abraham Lincoln, who grew up in a log cabin, was the 16th president of the US." Again, once students can create sentences with embedded clauses, they can recognize them more easily in a passage, which will lead to improved reading comprehension.

- **Combining sentences**—In *Writing Next*, Graham and Perin (2007) discuss the research supporting targeted work on sentence combining as an instructional activity for improving writing. They recommend teaching students how to construct complex sentences that link ideas with conjunctions, transition words, logical connectors, sequence terms, appositives, subordinate clauses, prepositional phrases, transition words, and more.

Remember sentence #4 at the start of this chapter? Bit by bit teachers can build students' writing muscles. Teachers might begin with helping students insert relative clauses. "John is wearing denim shorts" and "John sees an orange cat" could be combined as "John, who is wearing denim shorts, sees an orange cat" or "John, who sees an orange cat, is wearing denim shorts." Neither sentence is particularly academic nor very sensible out of context, but teachers might teach the process of sentence combining through simple sentences reflecting everyday concepts. After students use subordinate, embedded, or relative clauses to talk or write about people, places, and events that are familiar to them, they can apply that knowledge when discussing or writing about the content (e.g., "When we compare animals that live in the rain forest with those that live on the savanna, we find that the rain forest animals are smaller.").

We would suggest teachers continue a process like this to introduce students to a variety of ways to combine sentence ideas or add details, leading up to a smorgasbord activity, such as the following:

1. Provide a subject noun, verb, and object to start.

2. Have students add one or more modifiers (adjectives, adverbs).

---

[3] Our SIOP colleague, Amy Washam, gave us an example of a rule she heard a student identify: "Because sentences start with because, have two ideas that are separated by a comma, and the two ideas are related."

3. Have them add an adverb or adverbial phrase.

4. Have them add a conjunction and coordinating clause or a relative clause.

Additional steps may be added to the process depending on the age of your students. This kind of activity stretches students' level of writing and shows them precisely how to formulate more complex, interesting sentences.

ACTIVITY

Suppose a student has researched Nelson Mandela and created the following timeline:

1918 Nelson Mandela was born

1925 Nelson went to elementary school

1942 Mandela finishes a college degree with the University of South Africa

1943 Nelson studied law

1951 Elected President of African National Congress Youth League

1964 Found guilty at trial and sent to Robben Island

1990 Released from prison

1994 Elected as President of the Republic of South Africa

2013 Dies

A student might write a summary like this:

Nelson Mandela was born in 1918. He went to elementary school in 1925. He went to college and got a degree in 1942. He studied law in 1943. In 1951 Mandela was elected president of the African National Congress Youth League. In 1964 he was sent to prison on Robben Island. Mandela was released from prison in 1990. He was elected President of the Republic of South Africa in 1994. He died in 2013.

How would you help the student improve his writing?

Application to Common Core Standards

Our advanced learners will likely be in classes using state standards of English language arts, like the Common Core, as the basis for the curriculum and for the state ELA test. Writing is one area where these learners struggle to demonstrate proficiency. One of the Common Core ELA Anchor Standards for Writing is the following:

- Write narratives to develop real or imagined experiences or events using effective technique, relevant descriptive details, and well-structured event sequences.

This standard involves a high level of synthesis; in order to meet it, students must pull together knowledge of the narrative genre, skill in complex encoding to develop compelling paragraphs that include descriptive details, and the ability to use transitions and verb tenses to indicate event sequences.

Let's consider a lesson for a Grade 7 SIOP classroom. It is in the middle school grades that we find some of our long-term English learners. These students were part of the ESL program in elementary school but have not exited yet. For Grade 7, this standard is more specific:

- Use precise words and phrases, relevant descriptive details, and sensory language to capture the action and convey experiences and events.

In this Grade 7 lesson,[4] the students are editing a story they have already written. Several students in the class have passed the reading and oral language portions of the state English language proficiency text, but they have not mastered writing. The teacher is applying a vocabulary technique they have used in other lessons, Shades of Meaning, to help the class of English learners and native speakers improve the quality of their narratives.

Prior to the start of class, the teacher made a list of students according to their writing ability, from strongest to weakest. She then divided the list into two lists—with the better writers on one list and the weaker writers on the second—to purposefully pair the students. The strongest writer (on the first list) was paired with the student who headed the second list. The next strongest writer was paired with the second student on the second list, and so on.[5] In this way, the ability span between the pairs was fairly consistent.

The teacher began class by reviewing the lesson objectives. The content objective is

> Students will edit a peer's rough draft to identify overused or vague words.

The language objective is

> Peers (writer and editor) will discuss the selected words to generate and evaluate alternatives with more precision, description, or sensory detail.

After organizing the pairs in class, the teacher modeled the peer editing activity she was asking the students to do. Having noticed that much of the dialogue in the students' pieces was introduced with the word *said*, she began with that trite term. She read an example from a paper written in another class:

> The boy said, "Watch out!" as the car drove into the other lane.

and asked the students to say "Watch out!" to a partner. After listening to the class, the teacher asked a few students to describe the emotion of the expression as well as the loudness or softness of what they had just said. She then requested alternative words for *said*. Students offered *yelled*, *shouted*, and *screamed*. The class voted on the order that those words progressed in terms of intensity and the teacher wrote them on a replica of a paint chip worksheet. (See Figure 7.5.) She then read two more sentences and had students consider which of the three alternatives might suit this story the best.

Next, the teacher asked students if they could think of some other words that are not very descriptive or are used too much. Students suggested several, which she wrote on chart paper: *went, goes, asked, good, fine, nice, interesting, lots of,* and *really*. She encouraged the class to consult this chart while they edited their partner's story draft.

Figure 7.5 **Shades of Meaning for *Said***

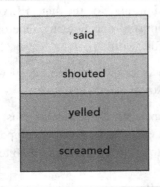

---

[4] Our thanks to Salvatora Bryk, an English language arts teacher at Nathan Hale Middle School in Norwalk, CT. This is a modification of her lesson plan.

[5] Suppose there were 10 students. A, B, C, D, and E were the top five writers in descending order. F, G, H, I, J were the lower five. A is paired with F, B with G, C with H, and so on.

She explained the task to the students and posted the directions.

1. Exchange story drafts with your partner.

2. Read your partner's story and identify words that are too simple, or over-used, or not explicit. Circle them.

3. Return the papers and review what your editor identified.

4. *Editor:* Share the words you selected with your partner. Try to agree on words to change. Give your reasons; listen to your partner's response.

5. Switch turns.

6. *Writer:* Once you have agreed on a set of words, write each of your words on paint chip worksheets (one per word).

7. Brainstorm together possible alternatives. Use a dictionary or thesaurus, if desired. Write these alternatives down, in order of intensity, on the paint chip worksheets. You can take turns or do one partner's words first and then the other's.

8. *Writer:* Review your story and consider the alternative words from the Shades of Meaning list. Select a better word and mark it on your draft. Make sure the word you select makes sense for your story's situation.

The student partners worked together for the rest of the period. Five minutes before the end of the period the teacher pulled the class together to wrap up the lesson with the High Five technique. Students were to stand up with their revised draft in one hand, raise the other hand and walk around. At her signal, they would find a new partner and give that person a high five. These partners were to share two of their original words and the replacements they had chosen. They repeated this activity one additional time, and then the teacher reviewed the objectives with the class. As she read the statements aloud, the students indicated with one, two, or three fingers whether they mastered (1), made progress (2), or didn't make progress (3) on the objectives that day.

Summary

In order for English learners to move beyond their present level of performance, they need systematic, focused instruction in all areas of language development: reading, writing, speaking, and listening. We cannot be complacent. Students may reach a level of proficiency that is adequate for participation and even success in their subject area classes, but that should not be the endpoint of their language development. Our goal is to develop proficiency in our English learners that meets or comes close to native proficiency. If we don't keep pushing our students, they risk becoming struggling readers or long-term English learners.

As you plan instruction, keep the following points in mind:

- Remember that language development is a multifaceted endeavor. It involves receptive skills (reading and listening), productive skills (writing and speaking), and interactive skills (receptive and productive working together). Across those skills reside numerous elements of academic language that are each important contributors to academic language proficiency.

- Develop a language profile of each student that identifies gaps in academic English skills. Compare notes with other teachers who might provide useful information to supplement students' test results.

- Plan and implement interventions that are designed for the specific skills each student needs. Remember that students are wasting valuable academic time practicing skills that they have already attained. Academic language instruction is not "one size fits all."

- Extend oral practice opportunities by providing scaffolds for students such as language frames and exposure to a variety of genres. Just as there are multiple genres of text, there are various genres of oral language use, and English learners will benefit from practice with them.

- Stretch students in the area of writing by demonstrating and then expecting higher levels of written expression from English learners.

Questions for Reflection

1. The notion of interactive language skills (receptive + productive) is a new concept. How would you explain it to a colleague? What examples might you provide?

2. Consider some students you know who are long-term English learners. What factors do you think led to their current status? What are some instructional or programmatic steps that can be taken to reduce the number of long-term English learners in the future?

3. Look at a language objective you have written recently. How can you ramp it up? Think about a language need your advanced level students have and modify that objective.

4. Read through the Guidelines for Advancing Language Proficiency in Figure 7.2. Which guidelines are most relevant for the students in your class? Discuss with a colleague some ideas for getting started. Which will you begin implementing first?

Appendix A: SIOP Protocol (Short Form)

The Sheltered Instruction Observation Protocol (SIOP)®

(Echevarria, Vogt, & Short, 2000, 2004, 2008, 2013, 2014a, 2014b)

Observer(s): _____   School: _____
Date: _____   Teacher: _____
Grade: _____   Class/Topic: _____
ESL Level: _____   Lesson: Multi-day Single-day (circle one)

Total Points Possible: 120 (subtract 4 points for each NA given) _____
Total Points Earned: _____   Percentage Score: _____

Directions: Circle the number that best reflects what you observe in a sheltered lesson. You may give a score from 0–4 (or NA on selected items). Cite under "Comments" specific examples of the behaviors observed.

Lesson Preparation

	Highly Evident		Somewhat Evident		Not Evident	
	4	3	2	1	0	N/A
1. **Content objectives** clearly defined, displayed, and reviewed with students	☐	☐	☐	☐	☐	
2. **Language objectives** clearly defined, displayed, and reviewed with students	☐	☐	☐	☐	☐	
3. **Content concepts** appropriate for age and educational background level of students	☐	☐	☐	☐	☐	
4. **Supplementary materials** used to a high degree, making the lesson clear and meaningful (e.g., computer programs, graphs, models, visuals)	☐	☐	☐	☐	☐	
5. **Adaptation of content** (e.g., text, assignment) to all levels of student proficiency	☐	☐	☐	☐	☐	☐
6. **Meaningful activities** that integrate lesson concepts (e.g., surveys, letter writing, simulations, constructing models) with language practice opportunities for reading, writing, listening, and/or speaking	☐	☐	☐	☐	☐	

Comments:

Building Background

	4	3	2	1	0	N/A
7. **Concepts explicitly linked** to students' background experiences	☐	☐	☐	☐	☐	☐
8. **Links explicitly made** between past learning and new concepts	☐	☐	☐	☐	☐	
9. **Key vocabulary** emphasized (e.g., introduced, written, repeated, and highlighted for students to see)	☐	☐	☐	☐	☐	

Comments:

Comprehensible Input

	4	3	2	1	0
10. **Speech** appropriate for students' proficiency level (e.g., slower rate, enunciation, and simple sentence structure for beginners)	☐	☐	☐	☐	☐
11. **Clear explanation** of academic tasks	☐	☐	☐	☐	☐
12. **A variety of techniques** used to make content concepts clear (e.g., modeling, visuals, hands-on activities, demonstrations, gestures, body language)	☐	☐	☐	☐	☐

Comments:

(continued)

SIOP Protocol *(Continued)*

	Highly Evident		Somewhat Evident		Not Evident	
Strategies	**4**	**3**	**2**	**1**	**0**	
13. Ample opportunities provided for students to use **learning strategies**	☐	☐	☐	☐	☐	
14. **Scaffolding techniques** consistently used assisting and supporting student understanding (e.g., think-alouds)	☐	☐	☐	☐	☐	
15. A variety of **questions or tasks that promote higher-order thinking skills** (e.g., literal, analytical, and interpretive questions)	☐	☐	☐	☐	☐	

Comments:

	4	**3**	**2**	**1**	**0**	**N/A**
Interaction						
16. Frequent opportunities for **interaction** and discussion between teacher/student and among students, which encourage elaborated responses about lesson concepts	☐	☐	☐	☐	☐	
17. **Grouping configurations** support language and content objectives of the lesson	☐	☐	☐	☐	☐	
18. Sufficient **wait time for student** responses consistently provided	☐	☐	☐	☐	☐	
19. Ample opportunities for students to **clarify key concepts in L1** as needed with aide, peer, or L1 text	☐	☐	☐	☐	☐	☐

Comments:

	4	**3**	**2**	**1**	**0**	**N/A**
Practice & Application						
20. **Hands-on materials and/or manipulatives** provided for students to practice using new content knowledge	☐	☐	☐	☐	☐	☐
21. Activities provided for students to **apply content and language knowledge** in the classroom	☐	☐	☐	☐	☐	☐
22. Activities integrate all **language skills** (i.e., reading, writing, listening, and speaking)	☐	☐	☐	☐	☐	

Comments:

	4	**3**	**2**	**1**	**0**
Lesson Delivery					
23. **Content objectives** clearly supported by lesson delivery	☐	☐	☐	☐	☐
24. **Language objectives** clearly supported by lesson delivery	☐	☐	☐	☐	☐
25. **Students engaged** approximately 90% to 100% of the period	☐	☐	☐	☐	☐
26. **Pacing** of the lesson appropriate to students' ability level	☐	☐	☐	☐	☐

Comments:

	4	**3**	**2**	**1**	**0**
Review & Assessment					
27. Comprehensive **review of key vocabulary**	☐	☐	☐	☐	☐
28. Comprehensive **review of key content concepts**	☐	☐	☐	☐	☐
29. Regular **feedback** provided to students on their output (e.g., language, content, work)	☐	☐	☐	☐	☐
30. **Assessment of student comprehension and learning** of all lesson objectives (e.g., spot checking, group response) throughout the lesson	☐	☐	☐	☐	☐

Comments:

Appendix B: Alignment of Common Core State Standards with the SIOP Model

CCSS & WIDA = *What* → SIOP Model = *How*

SIOP Model Features for Accessing the Common Core State Standards:

Lesson Preparation

1. Content objectives clearly defined, displayed, and reviewed with students *[Provide lesson purpose based on CCSS]*
2. Language objectives clearly defined, displayed, and reviewed with students *[Identify content specific academic language students need to learn and provide explicit instruction and practice]*
3. Content concepts appropriate for age and educational background *[Provide access to grade-level content using techniques for making content comprehensible]*
4. Supplementary materials used, making the lesson clear and meaningful *[Present content in diverse media and formats]*
5. Adaptation of content to all levels of student proficiency *[Provide differentiation for meeting lesson objectives]*
6. Meaningful activities that integrate lesson concepts with language practice opportunities for reading, writing, listening, and/or speaking *[Combine content and language learning opportunities to enhance lessons]*

Building Background

7. Concepts explicitly linked to students' background experiences *[Connect with what students know to make material relevant and meaningful]*
8. Explicitly link past learning and new concepts *[Help students recall relevant past learning and make connections to new information]*
9. Key vocabulary emphasized *[Provide explicit academic vocabulary instruction]*

Comprehensible Input

10. Use speech appropriate for students' proficiency level (e.g., slower rate, enunciation, and simple sentence structure for beginners) *[Adjust speech and word choice to advance student learning but not leave them behind]*
11. Explain academic tasks clearly *[Make expectations clear and teach task routines to students]*
12. A variety of techniques to make content concepts clear *[Provide appropriate instructional support for students' language proficiencies]*

Strategies

13. Ample opportunities provided for students to use learning strategies, (e.g., problem solving, predicting, organizing, summarizing, categorizing, evaluating, self-monitoring) *[Provide instruction in strategy use for accessing complex texts, determining unfamiliar vocabulary, planning and organizing ideas]*

Source: Echevarria, Short, & Vogt, 2013

14. Scaffolding techniques consistently used *[Offer support for advancing learning and for developing English proficiency]*
15. A variety of question types including those that promote higher-order thinking skills throughout the lesson *[Tap students' critical thinking skills and frames of reference through questioning and tasks]*

Interaction

16. Frequent opportunities for interaction and discussion between teacher/student and among students, which encourage elaborated responses about lesson concepts
17. Grouping configurations support language and content objectives of the lesson *[**For both above:** Provide informal discussion where students collaborate to answer questions, build understanding, present arguments, provide evidence, and solve problems]*
18. Provide sufficient wait time for student responses consistently *[English learners may need more time to compose their responses than native English speakers]*
19. Ample opportunities for students to clarify key concepts in L1 *[Use L1 as a resource for making CCSS lessons understandable]*

Practice & Application

20. Provide hands-on materials and/or manipulatives for students to practice using new content knowledge
21. Activities provided for students to apply content and language knowledge in the classroom
22. Activities integrate all language skills (i.e., reading, writing, listening, and speaking) *[**For all above:** Integrate and evaluate information; present information, findings and supporting evidence; use media and visual displays of data]*

Lesson Delivery

23. Support content objectives clearly *[Ensure lesson teaches to and/or practices stated content goals]*
24. Support language objectives clearly *[Ensure lesson teaches to and/or practices stated language goals]*
25. Students engaged approximately 90–100% of the period *[Ensure that students gain adequate exposure to a range of texts and tasks]*
26. Pacing of the lesson appropriate to the students' English proficiency levels *[Provide additional time as needed]*

Review & Assessment

27. Give a comprehensive review of key vocabulary *[Focus on key academic vocabulary]*
28. Give a comprehensive review of key content concepts *[Have students determine important learnings from the lesson]*
29. Provide feedback to students regularly on their output (e.g., language, content, work) *[Guide students as they strive for higher levels of understanding and language use]*
30. Assessment of student comprehension and learning of all lesson objectives (e.g., spot checking, group response) throughout the lesson *[Use multiple indicators to ensure comprehension and advance learning]*

Appendix C: SIOP Professional Development Resources

Books

Core SIOP Texts:

Echevarría, J., Short, D., & Peterson, C. (2012). *Using the SIOP® Model with pre-K and kindergarten English learners.* Boston: Allyn & Bacon.

Echevarría, J., Vogt, M.E., & Short, D. (2013). *Making content comprehensible for English learners: The SIOP® Model.* Fourth Edition. Boston: Allyn & Bacon.

Echevarría, J., Vogt, M.E., & Short, D. (2014a). *Making content comprehensible for elementary English learners: The SIOP® Model.* Second Edition. Boston: Allyn & Bacon.

Echevarría, J., Vogt, M.E., & Short, D. (2014b). *Making content comprehensible for secondary English learners: The SIOP® Model.* Second Edition. Boston: Allyn & Bacon.

Additional SIOP Texts:

Echevarría, J., Short, D., & Vogt, M.E. (2008). *Implementing the SIOP® Model through effective professional development and coaching.* Boston: Allyn & Bacon.

Echevarría, J., Vogt, M.E., & Short, D. (2010). *The SIOP® Model for teaching mathematics to English learners.* Boston: Allyn & Bacon.

Short, D., Echevarría, J., & Vogt, M.E. (2008). *The SIOP® Model for administrators.* Boston: Allyn & Bacon.

Short, D., Vogt, M.E., & Echevarría, J. (2011a). *The SIOP® Model for teaching history–social studies to English learners.* Boston: Allyn & Bacon.

Short, D., Vogt, M.E., & Echevarría, J. (2011b). *The SIOP® Model for teaching science to English learners.* Boston: Allyn & Bacon.

Vogt, M.E., & Echevarría, J. (2008). *99 ideas and activities for teaching English learners with the SIOP® Model.* Boston: Allyn & Bacon.

Vogt, M.E., Echevarría, J., & Short, D. (2010). *The SIOP® Model for teaching English–language arts to English learners.* Boston: Allyn & Bacon.

Vogt, M.E., Echevarría, J., & Washam, M.A. (2015). *99 MORE ideas and activities for teaching English learners with the SIOP® Model.* Boston: Allyn & Bacon.

Teaching English Learners with Learning Challenges:

Echevarría, J., & Graves, A. (2015). *Sheltered content instruction: Teaching English learners with diverse abilities.* Fifth Edition. Boston: Allyn & Bacon.

Echevarría, J., Richards-Tutor, C., & Vogt, M.E. (2015). *RTI and English learners: Using the SIOP Model.* Second Edition. Boston: Allyn & Bacon.

Journal Articles and Book Chapters

Echevarría, J., & Colburn, A. (2006). Designing lessons: Inquiry approach to science using the SIOP® Model. In A. Fathman & D. Crowther (Eds.), *Science for English language learners* (pp. 95–108). Arlington, VA: National Science Teachers Association Press.

Echevarría, J., Richards-Tutor, C., Canges, R., & Francis, D. (2011). Using the SIOP Model to promote the acquisition of language and science concepts with English learners. *Bilingual Research Journal, 34*(3), 334–351.

Echevarría, J., Richards-Tutor, C., Chinn, V., & Ratleff, P. (2011). Did they get it? The role of fidelity in teaching English learners. *Journal of Adolescent and Adult Literacy, 54*(6), 425–434.

Echevarría, J., & Short, D. (2004). Using multiple perspectives in observations of diverse classrooms: The Sheltered Instruction Observation Protocol (SIOP). In H. Waxman, R. Tharp, & S. Hilberg (Eds.), *Observational research in U.S. classrooms: New approaches for understanding cultural and linguistic diversity*. Boston: Cambridge University Press.

Echevarría, J., & Short, D. (2010). Programs and practices for effective sheltered content instruction. In California Department of Education (Ed.), *Improving education for English learners: Research-based approaches* (pp. 250–321). Sacramento, CA: CDE Press.

Echevarría, J., Short, D., & Powers, K. (2006). School reform and standards-based education: An instructional model for English language learners. *Journal of Educational Research, 99*(4), 195–210.

Echevarría, J., Short, D., Richards-Tutor, C., & Himmel, J. (In press). Using the SIOP Model as a professional development framework for comprehensive schoolwide intervention. In J. Echevarría, S. Vaughn, & D. Francis (Eds.). *English learners in content area classes: Teaching for achievement in the middle grades*. Boston: Allyn & Bacon.

Echevarría, J., & Vogt, M.E. (2010). Using the SIOP® Model to improve literacy for English learners. *New England Reading Association Journal (NERAJ), 46* (1) 8–15.

Guarino, A.J., Echevarría, J., Short, D., Schick, J.E., Forbes, S., & Rueda, R. (2001). The Sheltered Instruction Observation Protocol. *Journal of Research in Education, 11*(1), 138–140.

Kareva, V., & Echevarria, J. (2013). Using the SIOP Model for effective content teaching with second and foreign language learners. *Journal of Education and Training Studies, 1*(2), 239–248.

Short, D. (2013). Training and sustaining effective teachers of sheltered instruction. *Theory Into Practice, 52(2),* 118–127.

Short, D., Cloud, N., Morris, P., & Motta, J. (2012). Cross-district collaboration: Curriculum and professional development. *TESOL Journal, 3*(3), 402–424.

Short, D., & Echevarría, J. (2004/2005). Teacher skills to support English language learners. *Educational Leadership, 62*(4), 8–13.

Short, D., Echevarría, J., & Richards-Tutor, C. (2011). Research on academic literacy development in sheltered instruction classrooms. *Language Teaching Research, 15*(3), 363–380.

Short, D., Fidelman, C., & Louguit, M. (2012). Developing academic language in English language learners through sheltered instruction. *TESOL Quarterly, 46*(2), 333–360.

Vogt, M.E. (2012). English learners: Developing their literate lives. In R.M. Bean & A.S. Dagen (Eds.), *Best practice of literacy leaders: Keys to school improvement*. New York: The Guilford Press, 248–260.

Research Briefs (Downloadable)

Echevarria, J. (2012). *Effective practices for increasing the achievement of English learners.* Washington, DC: Center for Research on the Educational Achievement and Teaching of English Language Learners. Retrieved from *http://www.cal.org/create/resources/pubs/*

Echevarría, J., & Hasbrouck, J. (2009). *Response to intervention and English learners.* Washington, DC: Center for Research on the Educational Achievement and Teaching of English Language Learners. Retrieved from *http://www.cal.org/create/resources/pubs/responsetointerv.html*

Echevarría, J., & Short, D. (2011). *The SIOP® Model: A professional development framework for comprehensive school-wide intervention.* Washington, DC: Center for Research on the Educational Achievement and Teaching of English Language Learners. Retrieved from *http://www.cal.org/create/resources/pubs/professional-development-framework.html*

Himmel, J., Short, D.J., Richards, C., & Echevarría, J. (2009). *Using the SIOP® Model to improve middle school science instruction.* Washington, DC: Center for Research on the Educational Achievement and Teaching of English Language Learners. Retrieved from *http://www.cal.org /create/resources/pubs/siopscience.htm*

References

Adger, C.T., Snow, C.E., & Christian, D. (Eds.). (2002). *What teachers need to know about language.* Washington, DC: Center for Applied Linguistics.

Alvermann, D.E., & Moore, D.W. (2011). Questioning the separation of in-school from out-of-school contexts for literacy learning: An interview with Donna E. Alvermann. *Journal of Adolescent & Adult Literacy, 55*(2), 156–158.

Alves, M., Berman, M., & Gonzales, R. (2012). *The corpus-based word combination card.* Second Edition. Rockville, MD: Language Arts Press.

Anderson, L. W. & Krathwohl, D.R. (Eds.). (2001). *Taxonomy for learning, teaching, and assessing: A revision of Bloom's Taxonomy of Educational Objectives.* Boston, MA: Longman.

Anstrom, K., DiCerbo, P., Butler, F., Katz, A., Millet, J., & Rivera, C. (2010). *A review of the literature on Academic English: Implications for K–12 English Language Learners.* Arlington, VA: The George Washington University Center for Equity and Excellence in Education.

Applebee, A.N. (1984). Writing and reasoning. *Review of Educational Research, 54*(4), 577–596.

Applebee, A., Langer, J., Nystrand, M., & Gamoran, A. (2003). Discussion-based approaches to developing understanding: Classroom instruction and student performance in middle and high school English. *American Educational Research Journal, 40*(3), 685.

Arreaga-Mayer, C., & Perdomo-Rivera, C. (1996). Ecobehavioral analysis of instruction for at-risk language-minority students. *The Elementary School Journal, 96*(3), 245–258.

Ashcraft, N., & Tran, A. (Eds.). (2010). *Listening: TESOL classroom practice series.* Alexandria, VA: TESOL.

August, D., Artzi, L., & Mazrum, J. (2010). *Improving science and vocabulary learning of English language learners.* CREATE Brief. Washington, DC: Center for Research on the Education and Teaching of English Language Learners. Available fromt www.cal.org /create/publications/briefs/improving-science-and-vocabulary-learning-of-english-language-learners.html

August, D., & Shanahan, T. (Eds.). (2006). *Developing literacy in second-language learners: A report of the National Literacy Panel on Language-Minority Children and Youth.* Mahwah, NJ: Lawrence Erlbaum Associates.

August, D., & Shanahan, T. (2008). *Developing reading and writing in second-language learners.* New York, NY: Routledge.

Batt, E. (2010). Cognitive coaching: A critical phase in professional development to implement sheltered instruction. *Teaching and Teacher Education 26,* 997–1005.

Beck, I.L., McKeown, M.G., & Kucan, L. (2002). *Bringing words to life: Robust vocabulary instruction.* New York, NY: Guilford.

Benjamin, A., & Crow, J. (2013). *Vocabulary at the core: Teaching the Common Core standards.* New York, NY: Routledge.

Blachowicz, C.L., Fisher, P., Ogle, D.M., & Watts-Taffe, S. (2006). Vocabulary: Questions from the classroom. *Reading Research Quarterly, 41*(4), 524–539.

Brooks, K., & Thurston, L.P. (2010). English language learner academic engagement and instructional grouping configurations. *American Secondary Education, 39* (1), 45-60.

Buehl, D. (2009). *Classroom strategies for interactive learning.* Third Edition. Newark, DE: International Reading Association.

Butler, S., Urrutia, K., Buenger, A., Gonzalez, N., Hunt, M., & Eisenhart, D. (2010). *A review of current research on vocabulary instruction.* National Reading Technical Assistance Center, RMC Research Corporation.

California Department of Education. (2010). *Improving education for English learners: Research-based approaches.* Sacramento, CA: CDE Press. (See http://www.cde.ca.gov/re/pn for more information.)

Calkins, L. Ehrenworth, M., & Lehman, C. (2012). *Pathways to the Common Core.* Portsmouth, NH: Heinemann.

Carlo, M., August, D., McLaughlin, B., Snow, C., Dressler, C., Lippman, D., Lively, T., & White, C. (2004). Closing the gap: Addressing the vocabulary needs of English language learners in bilingual and mainstream classrooms. *Reading Research Quarterly, 39*(2), 188–215.

Cline, T., Crafter, S., O'Dell, L., & de Abreu, G. (2011). Young people's representations of language brokering. *Journal of Multilingual and Multicultural Development, 32*(3), 207–220.

Cloud, N., Genesee, F., & Hamayan, E. (2009). *Literacy instruction for English language learners: A teacher's guide to research-based practices.* Portsmouth, NH: Heinemann.

Cloud, N., Healey, K., Paul, M., Short, D., & Winiarski, P. (2010). Preparing adolescents for the academic listening demands of secondary school classrooms. In N. Ashcraft & A. Tran (Eds.), *Listening: TESOL classroom practice series* (pp. 151–167). Alexandria, VA: TESOL.

Cohen, A. (1998). *Strategies in learning and using a second language.* New York, NY: Longman.

Collier, V.P. (1987). Age and rate of acquisition of language for academic purposes. *TESOL Quarterly, 21*(4), 677.

Common Core Standards for English language arts and literacy (2010). Available from www.corestandards.org /ELA-literacy

Common Core Standards for Mathematics. (2010). Available from www.corestandards.org/Math

Cook, H.G., Boals, T., & Lundberg, T. (2011). Academic achievement for English language learners: What can we reasonably expect? *Phi Delta Kappan, 93*(2), 66–69.

Cook-Gumperz, J. (2006). *The social construction of literacy.* 2nd ed. Cambridge, UK: Cambridge University Press.

Cook-Gumperz, J. (Ed.). (2006). *The social construction of literacy.* Second Edition. Cambridge, UK: Cambridge University Press.

Coxhead, A. (2000). A new academic word list. *TESOL Quarterly, 34*(2): 213–238.

Cummins, J. (1981). The role of primary language development in promoting educational success for language minority students. In California State Department of Education (Ed.), *Schooling and language minority students: A theoretical framework* (pp. 3–49). Los Angeles: National Dissemination and Assessment Center.

Cunningham, A. (2005). Vocabulary growth through independent reading and reading aloud to children. In E.H. Hiebert & M.L. Kamil (Eds.), *Teaching and learning vocabulary: Bringing research to practice.*(pp. 48–68) Mahwah, NJ: Erlbaum.

Dalton, S. (2007). *Five standards for effective teaching: How to succeed with all learners, grades K–8.* San Francisco: Jossey-Bass.

DeLeeuw, H. (2008). *English language learners in Washington State.* Executive Summary. Report to the Washington State Board of Education, Olympia, WA, January 10, 2008.

Dressler, C., Carlo, M., Snow, C., August, D., & White, C. (2011). Spanish-speaking students' use of cognate knowledge to infer the meaning of English words. *Bilingualism, Language and Cognition 14*(2), 243–255.

Echevarría, J. (1995). Interactive reading instruction: A comparison of proximal and distal effects of instructional conversations. *Exceptional Children, 61*(6) 536–552.

Echevarría, J., & Graves, A. (2015). *Sheltered content instruction: Teaching English learners with diverse abilities.* Fifth Edition. Boston, MA: Allyn & Bacon.

Echevarría, J., Richards-Tutor, C., Canges, R., & Francis, D. (2011). Using the SIOP Model to promote the acquisition of language and science concepts with English learners. *Bilingual Research Journal, 34*(3), 334–351.

Echevarría, J., Short, D., & Peterson, C. (2012). *Using the SIOP model with pre-K and kindergarten English learners.* Boston, MA: Allyn & Bacon.

Echevarría, J., Short, D., & Powers, K. (2006). School reform and standards-based education: An instructional model for English language learners. *Journal of Educational Research, 99*(4), 195–211.

Echevarría, J., Vogt, M.E., & Short, D. (2010). *The SIOP® Model for teaching mathematics to English learners.* Boston, MA: Pearson Allyn & Bacon.

Echevarría, J., Vogt, M.E., & Short, D. (2013). *Making content comprehensible for English learners: The SIOP® Model.* Fourth Edition. Boston, MA: Pearson/Allyn & Bacon.

Echevarría, J., Vogt, M.E., & Short, D. (2014a). *Making content comprehensible for elementary English learners: The SIOP® model.* Second Edition. Boston, MA: Pearson Allyn & Bacon.

Echevarría, J., Vogt, M.E., & Short, D. (2014b). *Making content comprehensible for secondary English learners: The SIOP® model.* Second Edition. Boston, MA: Pearson Allyn & Bacon.

Fisher, D., & Frey, N. (2008). *Word wise and content rich.* Portsmouth, NH: Heinemann.

Fisher, D., Brozo, W.G., Frey, N., & Ivey, G. (2007). *50 content area strategies for adolescent literacy.* Upper Saddle River, NJ: Pearson/Merrill Prentice Hall.

Frazier, D. (2007). *Miss Alaineous: A vocabulary disaster.* Boston, MA: Houghton Mifflin Harcourt.

Freeman, Y., & Freeman, D. (2002). *Closing the achievement gap: How to reach limited formal schooling and long-term English learners.* Portsmouth, NH: Heinemann.

Friend, J., Most, R., & McCrary, K. (2009). The impact of a professional development program to improve urban middle-level English language learner achievement. *Middle Grades Research Journal, 4*(1), 53–75.

Fukkink, R.G., & de Glopper, K. (1998). Effects of instruction in deriving word meaning from context: A meta-analysis. *Review of Educational Research 68,* 450–469.

García, E. (2001). *Understanding and meeting the challenge of student diversity.* Third Edition. Boston, MA: Houghton Mifflin.

Genesee, F., Lindholm-Leary, K., Saunders, W., & Christian, D. (Eds.). (2006). *Educating English language learners: A synthesis of research evidence.* New York, NY: Cambridge University Press.

Gersten, R., Baker, S.K., Shanahan, T., Linan-Thompson, S., Collins, P., & Scarcella, R. (2007). *Effective literacy and English language instruction for English learners in the elementary grades: A practice guide* (NCEE 2007-4011). Washington, DC: National Center for Education Evaluation and Regional Assistance, Institute of Education Sciences, U.S. Department of Education. Available from http://ies.ed.gov/ncee/wwc/publications /practiceguides

Geva, E., & Yaghoub Zadeh, Z. (2006). Reading efficiency in native English-speaking and English-as-a-second-language children: The role of oral proficiency and underlying cognitive-linguistic processes. *Scientific Studies of Reading, 10,* 31–58.

Gibbons, P. (2002). *Scaffolding language, scaffolding learning.* Portsmouth, NH: Heinemann.

Gillanders, C., Castro, D. & Franco, F. (2014) Learning words for life: Promoting vocabulary in dual language learners. *The Reading Teacher, 68,* 3, 213–221.

Glick, J.E., & White, M.J. (2004). Post-secondary school participation of immigrant and native youth: The role of familial resources and educational expectations. *Social Science Research, 33,* 272–299.

Goldenberg, C. (2008). Teaching English language learners: What the research does—and does not—say. *American Educator, 32,* 2, 8-23, 42–44.

Graham, S., Bollinger, A., Booth Olson, C., D'Aoust, C., MacArthur, C., McCutchen, D., & Olinghouse, N. (2012). *Teaching elementary school students to be effective writers: A practice guide* (NCEE 2012- 4058). Washington, DC: National Center for Education Evaluation and Regional Assistance, Institute of Education Sciences, U.S. Department of Education. Available from http://ies.ed.gov/ncee/wwc/publications_reviews.aspx#pubsearch

Graham, S., & Perin, D. (2007). *Writing next: Effective strategies to improve writing of adolescents in middle and high schools.* Report to Carnegie Corporation of New York. Washington, DC: Alliance for Excellent Education.

Graves, M. (2006). *The vocabulary book: Learning & instruction.* New York, NY: Teachers College Press.

Graves, M.F., August, D., & Mancilla-Martinez, J. (2013). *Teaching vocabulary to English language learners.* New York: Teachers College Press.

Guglielmi, R. (2008). Native language proficiency, English literacy, academic achievement, and occupational attainment in limited-English-proficient students: A latent growth modeling perspective. *Journal of Educational Psychology, 100*(2), 322–342.

Hakuta, K., Butler, Y., & Witt, D. (2000). *How long does it take English learners to attain proficiency?* Policy Report 2000–1. Santa Barbara, CA: University of California, Linguistic Minority Research Institute.

Halgunseth, L. (2003). Language brokering: Positive developmental outcomes. In M. Coleman & L. Ganong (Eds.), *Points and counterpoints: Controversial relationship and family issues in the 21st century: An anthology* (pp. 154–157). Los Angeles, CA: Roxbury.

Halliday, M.A.K. (1994). *Introduction to functional grammar.* Second Edition. London: Edward Arnold.

Hasbrouck, J., & Tindal, G. A. (2006). Oral reading fluency norms: A valuable assessment tool for reading teachers. *The Reading Teacher, 59*(7), 636–644.

Helman, L., Bear, D., Invernizzi, M., Templeton, S., & Johnston, F. (2011). *Words their way with English learners: Word study for spelling, phonics and vocabulary.* Second Edition. Boston, MA: Pearson.

Herrell, A., & Jordan, M. (2008). *Fifty strategies for teaching English language learners.* Third Edition. Upper Saddle River, NJ: Pearson/Merrill Prentice Hall.

Hiebert, E., & Kamil, M. (Eds.). (2005). *Teaching and learning vocabulary: Bringing research to practice.* Mahwah, NJ: Erlbaum.

Himmel, J., Short, D., Echevarría, J., & Richards-Tutor, C. (2012). *Chemical interactions: Atoms and bonding unit.* Washington, DC: Center for Applied Linguistics and Cal State University, Long Beach Available from www.cal.org/create/pdfs/siop-atoms-and-bonding-unit.pdf

Hinkel, E. (2006). Current perspectives on teaching the four skills. *TESOL Quarterly 40*(1), 109–131.

Hoffman, J. (1992). Critical reading/thinking across the curriculum: Using I-charts to support learning. *Language Arts, 69*(2), 121–127.

Layne, S. (2015). *In defense of read-aloud: Sustaining best practice.* Portland, ME: Stenhouse Publishers.

Lesaux, N., Kieffer, M., Faller, J., & Kelley, J. (2010). The effectiveness and ease of implementation of an academic vocabulary intervention for linguistically diverse students in urban middle schools. *Reading Research Quarterly, 45*(2), 196–228.

Lesaux, N.K., Crosson, A., Kieffer, M.J., & Pierce, M. (2010). Uneven profiles: Language minority learners' word reading, vocabulary, and reading comprehension skills. *Journal of Applied Developmental Psychology, 31,* 475-483.

Lesaux, N.K., Kieffer, M.J., Kelley, J.G., & Harris, J.R. (2014). Effects of academic vocabulary instruction for linguistically diverse adolescents: Evidence from a randomized field trial. *American Educational Research Journal, 51*(6), 1159-1194

Lindholm-Leary, K., & Borsato, G. (2006). Academic achievement. In F. Genesee, K. Lindholm-Leary, W. Saunders, & D. Christian (Eds.), *Educating English language learners: A synthesis of research evidence* (pp. 176–221). New York: Cambridge University Press.

Lindholm-Leary, K., & Genesee, F. (2010). Alternative educational programs for English learners. In California Department of Education (2010), *Improving education for English learners: Research-based approaches* (pp. 323–382). Sacramento, CA: CDE Press.

Liu, D. (2012). The most frequently-used multi-word constructions in academic written English: A multi-corpus study. *English for Specific Purposes, 31*, 25–35.

Lubliner, S., & Hiebert, E.H. (2011). An analysis of English-Spanish cognates as a source of general academic language. *Bilingual Research Journal, 34*(1), 76–93.

Marzano, R., & Pickering, D. (2005). *Building academic vocabulary.* Teacher's manual. Alexandria, VA: Association for Supervision and Curriculum Development.

Marzano, R., Pickering, D., & Pollock, J. (2012). *Classroom instruction that works.* Second Edition. Alexandria, VA: Association for Supervision and Curriculum Development.

McIntyre, E., Kyle, D., Chen, C., Muñoz, M., & Beldon, S. (2010). Teacher learning and ELL reading achievement in sheltered instruction classrooms: Linking professional development to student development, *Literacy Research and Instruction, 49*(4), 334–351.

Menken, K. & Kleyn, T. (2009, April). The difficult road for long-term English learners. *Educational Leadership, 66*(7). Available online at www.ascd.org /publications/educational_leadership/apr09/vol66/ num07/The_Difficult_Road_for_Long-Term_English_ Learners.aspx

Mergendoller, J.R., Maxwell, N.L., & Bellisimo, Y. (2006). The effectiveness of problem-based instruction: A comparative study of instructional methods and student characteristics. *Interdisciplinary Journal of Problem-based Learning, 1*(2), 49–69.

Moje, E., Ciechanowski, K., Kramer, K., Ellis, L., Carrillo, R., & Collazo, T. (2004). Working toward third space in content area literacy: An examination of everyday funds of knowledge and discourse. *Reading Research Quarterly, 39*, 38–70.

Moschkovich, J. (2007). Examining mathematical discourse practices. *For the Learning of Mathematics, 27*, 24–30.

Nagy, W. E., & Anderson, R. C. (1984). How many words are there in printed English? *Reading Research Quarterly, 19*, 304–330.

Nagy, W. E., & Scott, J. A. (2000). Vocabulary processes. In M. Kamil, P. Mosenthal, P.D. Pearson, & R. Barr (Eds.), *Handbook of reading research* (vol. 3, pp. 269–284). Mahwah, NJ: Erlbaum.

Nagy, W. E., & Townsend, D. (2012). Words as tools: Learning academic vocabulary as language acquisition. *Reading Research Quarterly, 47* (1), 91–108.

NGSS Lead States. (2013). Next generation science standards: For states, by states. Washington, DC: The National Academies Press.

National Council for Teachers of Mathematics. (1989). *Curriculum and evaluation standards for school mathematics.* Reston, VA: Author.

National Governors Association, Center for Best Practices and Council of Chief State School Officers. (2010a). *Common core state standards for English language arts and literacy in history/social studies, science, and technical subjects.* Washington, DC: Author.

National Governors Association, Center for Best Practices and Council of Chief State School Officers. (2010b). Common core state standards for mathematics. Washington, DC: Author.

National Institute of Child Health and Human Development (NICHD). (2000). *Report of the National Reading Panel. Teaching children to read: An evidence-based assessment of the scientific research literature on reading and its implications for reading instruction.* (NIH Publication No. 00–4769). Washington, DC: U.S. Department of Health and Human Services.

New York City Department of Education. (2004). *The class of 2000 final longitudinal report: A three year follow-up study.* New York, NY: New York City Department of Education, Division of Assessment and Accountability.

Nieto, S., & Bode, P. (2011). *Affirming diversity.* Sixth Edition. Boston, MA: Pearson.

Nilep, C. (2006). "Code Switching" in sociocultural linguistics. *Colorado Research in Linguistics, 19*, 1–22.

Olson, L. (2101). *Reparable harm: Fulfilling the unkept promise of educational opportunity for California's long term English learners.* Long Beach, CA: Californians Together.

Palinscar, A.C., & Brown, A.L. (1984). Reciprocal teaching of comprehension-fostering and comprehension-monitoring activities. *Cognition and Instruction, 1*, 117–175.

Parent, K. (2009). *Polysemy: A second language pedagogical concern.* Unpublished dissertation. Victoria University of Wellington, Wellington, New Zealand. Retrieved from http://researcharchive.vuw.ac.nz/bitstream /handle/10063/970/thesis.pdf?sequence=1

Perez, E. (1981). Oral language competence improves reading skills of Mexican American third graders. *Reading Teacher, 35*, 24–27.

Rance-Roney, J. (2010). Jump-starting language and schema for English language learners: Teacher-composed digital jump-starts for academic reading. *Journal of Adolescent & Adult Literacy, 53*(5), 386–395.

Readance, J.E., Bean, T.W., & Baldwin, R.S. (2012). *Content area literacy: An integrated approach.* Twelfth Edition. Dubuque, IA: Kendall /Hunt.

Resnick, L., & Snow, C. (2009). *Speaking and listening for preschool through third grade.* Newark, DE: International Reading Association.

Restrepo, M., & Gray, S. (2007). Optimizing literacy in English language learners. *Seminars in Speech and Language, 28*(1), 25–34.

Reutebuch, C. (2010). Effective social studies instruction to promote the knowledge acquisition and vocabulary learning of English language learners in the middle grades. CREATE Brief. Washington, DC: Center for Applied Linguistics. Available from www.cal.org/create/publications/briefs/effective-social-studies-instruction.html

Riches, C., & Genesee, F. (2006). Literacy: Crosslinguistic and crossmodal issues. In F. Genesee, K. Lindholm-Leary, W. Saunders, & D. Christian (Eds.), *Educating English language learners: A synthesis of research evidence* (pp. 64–108). New York, NY: Cambridge University Press.

Ruddell, M.R., & Shearer, B.A. (2002). "Extraordinary," "tremendous," "exhilarating," "magnificent": Middle school at-risk students become avid word learners with the Vocabulary Self-Collection Strategy (VSS). *Journal of Adolescent and Adult Literacy, 45*(4), 352–363.

Saunders, W., & Goldenberg, C. (2010). Research to guide English language development instruction. In California Department of Education (Ed.), *Improving education for English learners: Research-based approaches* (pp. 22–81). Sacramento: CA Dept. of Education.

Saunders, W., & Marcelletti, D. (2013). The gap that can't go away: The catch-22 of reclassification in monitoring the progress of English learners. *Educational Evaluation and Policy Analysis, 35*(2), 139–156.

Saunders, W., & O'Brien, G. (2006). Oral language. In F. Genesee, K. Lindholm-Leary, W. Saunders, & D. Christian (Eds.), *Educating English language learners: A synthesis of research evidence* (pp. 14–63). New York, NY: Cambridge University Press.

Scott, J., & Nagy, W. (2004). Developing word consciousness. In J.F. Bauman & E.J. Kame'enui (Eds.), *Vocabulary instruction: Research to practice* (pp. 201–217). New York, NY: Guilford Press.

Seedhouse, P., Walsh, S., & Jenks, C. (2010). *Conceptualizing 'learning' in applied linguistics.* London: Palgrave Macmillan.

Seidlitz, J. (2008). *Navigating the ELPS.* San Antonio, TX: Canter Press.

Seidlitz, J., & Perryman, B. (2011). *7 steps to a language-rich interactive classroom.* San Antonio, TX: Canter Press.

Short, D. (2012). *Research on developing academic language and literacy in English language learners.* International Reading Association Conference presentation, Chicago, IL, May 1, 2012.

Short, D. (2013). Training and sustaining effective teachers of sheltered instruction. *Theory Into Practice, 52*(2), 118–127.

Short, D. (2014). *Long-term English learners: Identification and intervention.* [Presentation] Interrupting the Generational Cycle of ELL Symposium, Arlington Heights, IL, October 22, 2014.

Short, D., Echevarría, J., & Richards-Tutor, C. (2011). Research on academic literacy development in sheltered instruction classrooms. *Language Teaching Research, 15*(3), 363–380.

Short, D., Fidelman, C., & Louguit, M. (2012). Developing academic language in English language learners through sheltered instruction. *TESOL Quarterly 46*(2), 333–360.

Short, D., & Fitzsimmons, S. (2007). *Double the work: Challenges and solutions to acquiring language and academic literacy for adolescent English language learners.* Report to Carnegie Corporation of New York. Washington, DC: Alliance for Excellent Education.

Short, D., Vogt, M.E., & Echevarría, J. (2011a). *The SIOP ® Model for teaching history – social studies to English learners.* Boston, MA: Allyn & Bacon.

Short, D., Vogt, M.E., & Echevarría, J. (2011b). *The SIOP ® Model for teaching science to English learners.* Boston, MA: Allyn & Bacon.

Silverman, R., & Hines, S. (2009). The effects of multimedia-enhanced instruction on the vocabulary of English-language learners and non-English-language learners in pre-kindergarten through second grade. *Journal of Educational Psychology, 101*(2), 305–314.

Skerrett, A., & Bomer, R. (2011). Borderzones in adolescents' literacy practices: Connecting out-of-school literacies to the reading curriculum. *Urban Education, 46*(6), 1256–1279.

Smith, A. T., & Agnotti, R. T. (2012). "Why are there so many words in math?": Planning for content-area vocabulary instruction. *Voices from the Middle, 20*(1), 43–51.

Snow, C. E., & White, C. (2012). *Using discussable topics to teach vocabulary and academic language: Word Generation in English language arts classrooms.* Manuscript submitted for publication.

Snow, C., Lawrence, J., & White, C. (2009). Generating knowledge of academic language among urban middle school students. *Journal of Research on Educational Effectiveness, 2*, 325–344.

Snow, C.E., & Uccelli, P. (2009). The challenge of academic language. In D.R. Olson, & N. Torrance (Eds.), *The Cambridge Handbook of Literacy* (pp. 112–133). Cambridge, UK: Cambridge University Press.

Stahl, S., & Nagy, W. (2005). *Teaching word meanings.* Mahwah, NJ: Erlbaum.

Stanovich, K. (1986). Matthew effects in reading: Some consequences of individual differences in the acquisition of literacy. *Reading Research Quarterly, 21*(4), 360–407.

State of New Jersey Department of Education. (2006). *Preliminary analysis of former limited English proficient students' scores on the New Jersey language arts and literacy exam, 2005–2006*. Trenton, NJ: State of New Jersey Department of Education, New Jersey State Assessment Office of Title I.

Sullivan, P., Yeager, M., O'Brien, E., Kober, N., Gayler, K., Chudowsky, N., Chudowsky, V., Wooden, J., Jennings, J., &. Stark Rentner, D. (2005). *States try harder, but gaps persist: High school exit exams 2005*. Washington, DC: Center on Education Policy.

Tarone, E., & Bigelow, M. (2005). Impact of literacy on oral language processing: Implications for second language acquisition research. *Annual Review of Applied Linguistics, 25*, 77–97.

Tharp, R., & Gallimore, R. (1988). *Rousing minds to life: Teaching, learning, and schooling in social context*. New York, NY: Cambridge University Press.

Thomas, W.P., & Collier, V.P. (2002). *A national study of school effectiveness for language minority students' long-term academic achievement*. Santa Cruz, CA, and Washington, DC: Center on Research, Diversity & Excellence.

Uccelli, P. (2012). *Assessing academic language*. CREATE conference presentation at English Learners in Content-Area Classes: Teaching for Achievement in the Middle Grades, October 2012, Orlando, FL. Available from www.cal.org/create/conferences/2012/presentations-and-handouts.html

van Lier, L., & Walqui, A. (2012). *Language and the Common Core State Standards*. Retrieved January 22, 2014, from http://ell.stanford.edu/sites/default/files/pdf/academic-papers/04-Van%20Lier%20Walqui%20Language%20and%20CCSS%20FINAL.pdf

Vaughn, S., Martinez, L.R., Linan-Thompson, S., Reutebuch, C.K., Carlson, C.D., & Francis, D.J. (2009). Enhancing social studies vocabulary and comprehension for seventh-grade English language learners: Findings from two experimental studies. *Journal of Research on Educational Effectiveness, 2*(4), 297–324.

Verplaetse, L.S. (2001). How content teachers allocate turns to limited English proficient students. *Journal of Education, 183*(1), 19–35.

Vogt, M.E., & Echevarría, J. (2008). *99 ideas and activities for teaching English learners with the SIOP® Model*. Boston, MA: Allyn & Bacon.

Vogt, M.E., Echevarría, J., & Short, D. (2010). *Teaching English–language arts to English learners with the SIOP Model*. Boston, MA: Pearson Allyn & Bacon.

Vogt, M., Echevarria, J., & Washam, A. (2015). *99 MORE ideas and activities for teaching English learners with the SIOP Model*. Boston, MA: Pearson.

Vygotsky, , L. (1978). *Mind and society: The development of higher psychological processes* (M. Cole, V. John-Steiner, S. Scribner, & E. Souberman, Eds. and trans.). Cambridge, MA: Harvard University Press.

Wajnrib, R. (1990). *Grammar dictation*. Oxford, UK: Oxford University Press.

Watson, K., & Young, B. (1986). Discourse for learning in the classroom. *Language Arts, 63*(2), 126–133.

Webb, N.L. (1997). Determining alignment of expectations and assessment in math and science education. *NISE Brief, 1*(1), 1–8. National Institute for Science Education, University of Wisconsin, Madison.

White, T.G., Sowell, J., & Yanagihara, A. (1989). Teaching elementary students to use word part clues. *The Reading Teacher, 42*, 302–308.

Wiggins, G., & McTighe, J. (2008). Put understanding first. *Educational Leadership, 65*,(8), 36–41.

Wray, A. (2000). Formulaic sequences in second language teaching: Principle and practice. *Applied Linguistics, 21*, 463–489.

Xu, S. (2008). Rethinking literacy learning and teaching: Intersections of adolescents' in-school and out-of-school literacy practices. In K.A. Hinchman, & H.K. Sheridan-Thomas (Eds.), *Best practices in adolescent literacy instruction* (pp. 39–56). New York, NY: Guilford Press.

Zwiers, J. (2008). *Building academic language: Essential practices for content classrooms*. San Francisco, CA: John Wiley & Sons, Inc.

Zwiers, J., & Crawford, M. (2011). *Academic conversations: Classroom talk that fosters critical thinking and content understandings*. Portland, ME: Stenhouse.

Index